Alaska's

FOUNTAINHEA COLLECTION

VINTAGE TREADS AND THREADS

NANCY D. DeWITT

EDITED BY JOHN F. KATZ   PHOTOGRAPHY BY RONN MURRAY

FOUNTAINHEAD ANTIQUE AUTO MUSEUM AT WEDGEWOOD RESORT

For Treads and Threads lovers everywhere
and to the staff of Fountainhead Development,
who have enabled a dream to become a reality
—Tim Cerny

Editor: John F. Katz
Design: Elizabeth M. Watson, Watson Graphics
Publication management: Susan Dupere, Epicenter Press/Aftershocks Media

Library of Congress Control Number: 2011928201
ISBN 978-0-615-48145-6

Photo Credits:
Except as noted below, photographs were taken by Ronn Murray Photography, ©2011 Ronn Murray.
Deanna Brandon: 4, 8 (dress), 11, 14, 15 (far right), 17 (dresses), 19, 20, 22, 44 (upper left), 45, 50 (upper right), 51, 57, 61, 65, 74, 83, 85, 100 (far left), 105 (left), 120
Sean Brayton: 80, 81
Cass Cerny: 29, 35, 48 (left), 76 (dress), 79, 87, 100 (far right), 101 (right), 104 (left)
Nancy DeWitt: 5 (upper left, lower right), 30
Jody Thomas Photography: 56 (lower right)

Front cover photo: 1920 Argonne Model D Roadster

For more information about the publisher:
Fairbanks Antique Auto Museum
212 Wedgewood Drive
Fairbanks, Alaska 99701
(907) 450-2100
http://www.fountainheadmuseum.com
info@fountainheadmuseum.com

10 9 8 7 6 5 4 3 2 1
Printed in China

CONTENTS

7

99

107

INTRODUCTION

Tim and Barbara Cerny. 1912 Premier Model 4-40 Touring

In 1974, Tim Cerny purchased his first car—a 1951 Dodge Wayfarer. He could not have suspected that his new passion for older cars had set him on the road to founding an antique automobile museum in Alaska. Over the years, as he learned more about antique cars and the United States' colorful automotive history, he began to dream of accumulating a top-class collection of antique autos. The dream became reality when, in 2007, he purchased a significant portion of the J. Parker Wickham automobile collection. Tim's company, Fountainhead Development, broke ground for a new museum at Wedgewood Resort in Fairbanks the following spring.

For several years Tim and his colleagues researched and acquired additional cars from throughout North America and Europe. Each represented a significant or unusual development in American automotive technology or design, or was an extremely rare example of its marque or model. Other vehicles were selected for their Alaskan provenance, or for being examples of the earliest cars to reach Alaska. On June 1, 2009, the 30,000-square-foot Fountainhead Museum opened its doors, fulfilling Tim's desire to preserve these historical treasures and share them with the public.

The collection presently encompasses 78 vehicles, including the 42 featured in this book. They range from the obscure (Hertel, Compound and Argonne) to the legendary (Packard, Peerless and Pierce-Arrow), each exemplifying some of the most fascinating developments in U.S. automotive history prior to World War II. Remarkably, museum staff and volunteers drive all but a few of the cars each summer, making this a true "living museum."

While we recognize that definitions for automotive eras vary widely and lack rigid boundaries, the time periods selected for this book mirror those used to categorize our museum exhibits. Alaskan historic photos and

videos from these eras are displayed with the cars, vividly illustrating the extraordinary challenges faced by Alaska's pioneering motorists. Although horrendous road conditions and the severe climate were unkind to their vehicles, some of these early cars have survived and several are showcased in our Alaska Gallery.

Visitors to the Fountainhead Museum also discover how early 20th Century fashion was influenced by the automobile. Barbara Cerny, Tim's wife and curator of the textile collection, has assembled an extensive assortment of formal wear, everyday fashions, motoring clothes and accessories, including pieces from Alaska's pioneers. Together, the automobiles, photographs and fashions illustrate how technology, culture and style evolved as America fell in love with newfound speed and mobility provided by the automobile.

Left top: 1904 Rambler Model L.
Left bottom: 1930 Packard Deluxe Eight Roadster.
Below: 2010 Midnight Sun Cruise-In. Firing up the 1909 Stanley Steam Car.

1. THE VETERAN ERA

1890s–1904

The Veteran Era spanned the fledgling years of the automobile, a time when horseless carriages were seen as more of an expensive novelty than a useful transportation device. Automobile development progressed haphazardly at first, as inventors operated with no consistent standards for basic vehicle architecture or materials—and often with insufficient capital to move into production. The few who succeeded included Ransom E. Olds, Henry Ford, Henry Leland and the Studebaker brothers.

One and two-cylinder engines, chain drive, tiller steering and wooden buggy bodies were the norm during this time, as were breakdowns and tire punctures. Electric and steam-driven automobiles were more popular than those powered by internal "explosion" engines. Closed cars were almost exclusively custom-built, expensive and extremely rare.

No automobiles reached Alaska during the Veteran Era. Instead, the Territory's pioneers relied on sternwheelers, horses, dog sleds, trains, bicycles and their own two feet for transportation.

Gibson Girl gown of very fine wool, velvet and lace (ca. 1902)

D.T. Kennedy's passenger sleds prepare to leave Valdez for the 365-mile journey to Fairbanks. John Zug Collection 80-0068-00053; Archives, University of Alaska Fairbanks

1898 HAY MOTOR VEHICLE

Stanhope Phaeton

This Hay Motor Vehicle is the oldest four-cylinder, internal combustion American automobile known to exist.

The Hay Motor Vehicle is an extraordinary example of a pre-1900 automobile. Compared to other early horseless carriages, this is a big, handsome and imposing car. The high quality of the carriage design, coachwork, wheels and metalwork is also remarkable for an automobile of this era. With the exception of the tires, every part was handcrafted specifically for this prototype, the only known Hay Motor Vehicle in existence.

Although seemingly ahead of its time, the Hay apparently never made it into production. Likely this was due to a flawed engine design that limited this prototype to a few short runs. The unusual—and essentially unusable—engine is an eight-cycle, horizontally opposed four that produces a firing stroke in each cylinder on every fourth turn. Inventor Walter Hay claimed that the eight-cycle concept provided two full revolutions to purge the cylinders of any remaining exhaust and allow them to cool. Fins radiating from each cylinder supplemented this internal cooling, but no water was used. Allegedly the Hay could operate without oil, "the motor simply running a trifle harder when no oil is used."

This Hay Motor Vehicle was discovered in a barn in the 1940s, not far from where it was built in New Haven, Connecticut. Over the past six decades, it has passed through several owners and spent many years in restoration. The Fountainhead Antique Auto Museum purchased the car in 2007 and spent two years completing its restoration to like-new condition.

1898 HAY MOTOR VEHICLE

1899 HERTEL

Runabout

Although cleverly engineered, the Hertel is basically an engine and body mounted between two bicycle frames.

The Hertel runabout, introduced in 1898, nicely illustrates the transition from bicycles to automobiles. Its front wheels are mounted to bicycle forks and steered by a tiller attached to the right front wheel. It has a simple tubular frame and metal-paneled body, which gave the Hertel "an air of strength and durability" according to its designer.

All four wheels pivot independently on short trailing arms—an idea way ahead of the Hertel's time. The centrally mounted hand lever controls the throttle and brakes, and engages the drive; it also functions as a starting lever in lieu of a crank. Instead of using belts, chains or gears, the two-cylinder engine drives friction pulleys that rotate against the inner rims of the rear wheels. Each of the two cylinders has a muffler, with one arranged to heat incoming air for vaporizing the gasoline. The manufacturer claimed the Hertel was odorless and "practically noiseless" as a result.

This is one of only three Hertels known to exist. It spent much of its life in museums and was restored only as necessary to keep it in operating condition. Many of its parts were hand-made, including the hand-forged ironwork of the suspension components.

1899 HERTEL

1903 TOLEDO

1903 TOLEDO

Rear-Entrance Touring Car

This is the sole internal-combustion-powered Toledo known to survive.

The American Bicycle Company became Toledo's first automobile manufacturer, introducing a steam runabout named after the city in 1901. By 1902, the renamed International Motor Car Company boasted "the largest automobile factory in the world." That same year they introduced their first "gasoline" (or, more properly, *internal combustion*) Toledo, which became a quick seller.

The internal-combustion Toledos of 1903 were eye-catching. The tapered bonnet was unusually long for a two-cylinder car to accommodate the large radiator tank in front of the engine. Wooden artillery wheels, white tires, a brass front screen, brass lamps and side-mounted wicker baskets added to its good looks. The optional fixed roof and roll-down side curtains offered passengers protection from inclement weather.

This award-winning Toledo has an interesting hill brake—essentially a pole that swings down from the chassis and digs into the ground—and

is one of the first cars to have an electric speedometer. Unlike the two-speed planetary transmissions found in most cars of the time, the 12-horsepower

(hp) Toledo had a three-speed sequentially shifted sliding-gear transmission.

In May of 1903, Colonel Albert Pope reorganized the International Motor Car Company as the Pope Motor Company. The steam cars were abandoned, but the internal-combustion cars continued as Pope-Toledos.

1903 TOLEDO

Fairbanks undertaker Hosea Ross with a load of live cargo in his Pierce Great Arrow touring car. PHOTO COURTESY OF CANDY WAUGAMAN

2. THE BRASS ERA

1905–1912

The Brass Era—named for the widespread use of brass trim, lights, and other accessories—was a time of tremendous growth and innovation for the American automotive industry. While hundreds, if not thousands, of hopeful automaking ventures lasted less than a year or two, names still familiar today such as Cadillac, Oldsmobile, and Packard firmly established themselves as leaders in the industry. More affordable cars from Buick, Ford, Overland and Maxwell surged even further ahead; now automobiles were no longer limited to the wealthy. The arrival of the electric starter in late 1911 hastened the demise of electric and steam-powered cars, but also allowed more women to take the wheel.

During this time the standard automobile evolved into a front-engined, usually four-cylinder internal-combustion device with rear-wheel drive. While Ford clung stubbornly to a planetary transmission, most others adopted sliding spur gears. Buggy-style bodies were largely replaced by lower, sleeker roadsters and touring cars. Led by Ford's Model T in late 1908, automakers began switching steering wheels to the left, although some would retain right-hand steering until 1920.

The first automobile appeared in Alaska in 1905, a crude runabout built by a man who had never seen a car before. In April 1908 the Thomas Flyer competing in the New York-Paris Race became the first car to reach Valdez, but deep snow prevented it from leaving the dock. Later that year three touring cars arrived by sternwheeler in Fairbanks. By 1912 Pope-Toledo, White Steamer, Franklin, Chalmers-Detroit, Pierce and Thomas Flyer were among the marques rolling on the streets of this Gold Rush town.

Tea or lingerie dresses of cotton, linen, cutwork and lace (ca. 1905-10)

1906 CADILLAC

Model K Runabout

Winner of the prestigious Dewar Trophy for its precision engineering.

I n 1903 Henry Leland introduced his first Cadillac, an attractive "one-lunger" that sold surprisingly well and quickly earned a reputation for reliability, driving simplicity, ease of maintenance, and remarkable pulling and climbing capability. The Victoria, or "tulip," body, in which the gracefully curved seat sides resembled a flower petal, became an immediate sensation when Cadillac introduced the Model K in 1906. Because under-seat engines were by then passé, Cadillac disguised the Model K with a dummy front hood that housed only the radiator and water tank.

While other cars of the time were heavy and expensive to run, the single-cylinder Cadillac was light, reliable and cheap to operate. The Model K was also quite fast for a one-cylinder car, helping Cadillac reach their highest single-cylinder production total of 3,650 cars in 1906.

Leland, who came from the arms industry, understood the importance of precision-engineered *interchangeable* parts that could be assembled without the hand-fitting that characterized most automobile manufacturing in the early 20th century. Cadillac made history, and earned the prestigious Dewar Trophy, in 1908 when the marque's London distributor disassembled three Model Ks, randomly mixed their parts with spare parts from inventory, and then re-assembled three working automobiles.

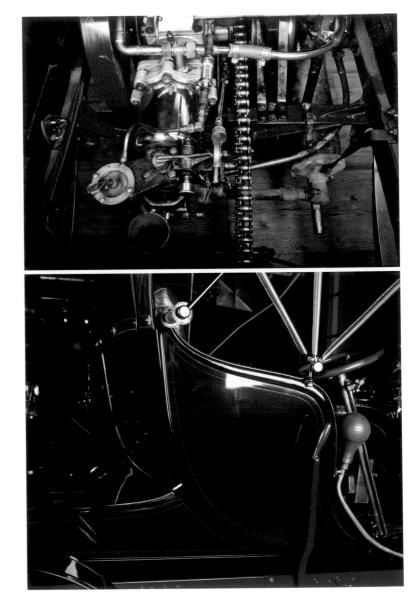

1906 CADILLAC

1906 COMPOUND

1906 COMPOUND

Model 7 ¹/₂ Light Touring

"Startling cool, quiet and odorless exhaust."

This is the only surviving example of a Compound, a car named for its unconventional internal-combustion engine that functioned similar to a compound steam engine. Only the outer two of the three cylinders fired in the usual manner. Rather than venting directly into the atmosphere, exhaust from these high-compression cylinders emptied into the center, low-pressure cylinder, where it expanded further and drove a third piston. This multiple expansion or "compounding" feature reportedly increased fuel economy and resulted in a cleaner and unusually quiet, cool and odorless final exhaust.

The Compound was one of the earliest cars to have power-assisted brakes, using a compressed-air servo acting on its otherwise conventional mechanical brake linkage. It was notable, also, for its unusual "Deadman Switch" mounted to the right of the driver. If the driver lifted his right arm off the switch (even to wave), the throttle would automatically shut off and the brakes would be applied.

Originally called the Graham-Fox, roughly 300 Compounds were manufactured by the Eisenhuth Horseless Vehicle (EHV) Company in Middletown, Connecticut between 1904 and 1908. This car's entire history can be traced back to original owner John Unser, the chief engineer and superintendent of the EHV Company and a key designer of the Compound.

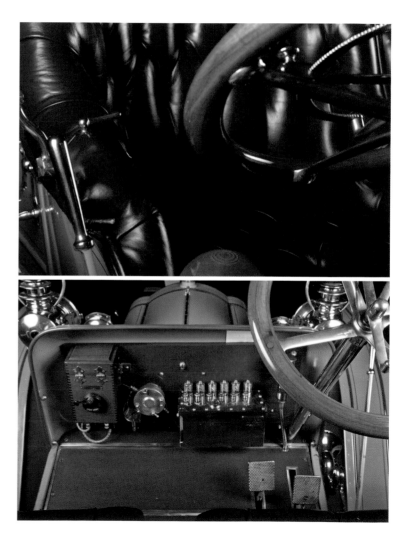

1907 CARTERCAR

1907 CARTERCAR

Model A Fixed Tonneau Five-Passenger Touring Car

The Cartercar was the most well-known and successful U.S. automobile to employ a friction-drive transmission.

Cartercar designer Byron Carter believed that the number of a car's drive speeds should be left up to the driver, not to the transmission. Instead of gears, his gearless transmission used friction discs. A hand lever

moved a perpendicular friction wheel across the face of a whirling drive disc to change speed—with faster "gearing" obtained as the wheel moved from the center toward the edge of the disc. Crossing over the center of the drive disc produced reverse. Just like a conventional transmission, the system could also be used to slow the car, simply by moving the friction wheel back toward the center of the drive disc.

Friction drive was simple, inexpensive to produce and virtually maintenance-free. It only required a little grease and replacement of the friction wheel's paper rim every 4,000 miles. Thus, the Cartercar was touted as "the simplest automobile in the world which even the most inexperienced operator cannot ruin or hurt. A thousand speeds, no clutch to slip, no gears to strip, no universal joints to break, no shaft drive to twist, no bevel gears to wear and howl, no noise to annoy."

Byron Carter died unexpectedly in 1908, and the following year the company was scooped up by General Motors. Fewer than 30 Cartercars are known to survive, including five 1907 models. This Model A is powered by a two-cylinder, horizontally opposed engine that displaces 214 cubic inches and develops 24 hp.

1907 FORD

Model K 6-40 Roadster

Henry Ford loathed the big, expensive Model K, as his goal was to build a light, reliable and affordable "car for the multitudes."

The upscale Model K was forced upon a reluctant Henry Ford by company directors determined to enter the lucrative luxury car market. It was the Ford Motor Company's first six-cylinder automobile, built at a time when the industry was just beginning to experiment with sixes. Conservatively rated 40 hp from 405 cubic inches, a stock Model K roadster could reach 60 mph. A stripped-down racer driven by Frank Kulick set a new 24-hour record of 1135 miles at 47.2 mph.

Although beautiful and fast, the big Ford was plagued by mechanical failures. Frame flex tortured the nickel-aluminum crankcase, causing breakage at the rear flange and mounting studs; on a very bad road the engine might lock up entirely. The overtaxed two-speed planetary transmission not only devoured brake bands, but occasionally regurgitated gears out through its casing. Only 900 Model Ks, including 50 roadsters, were produced from 1906 to 1908; and Henry Ford refused to even consider another six until 1941. But with its long hood and low profile, the Model K roadster accurately anticipated the suave, self-assured look of better-known big-engined American sports cars yet to come.

Fewer than 25 Model Ks, of which 10 are roadsters, are known to still exist. This roadster won the 1982 Veteran Motor Car Club of America Gold Cup and in 1982 was used

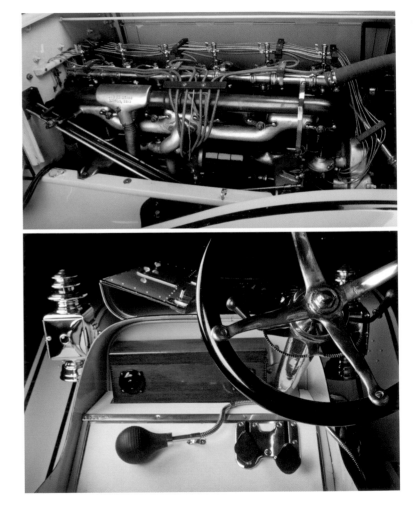

to reenact the start of the 1909 New York to Seattle Race. Its detachable "mother-in-law" seat can be removed and replaced with a storage trunk.

1907 FORD

1907 FRANKLIN

Type D Landaulet

A 1908 six-cylinder Franklin touring car was the second automobile to arrive in Fairbanks and the first to reach the mining camp of Dome. Franklins were touted as the ideal car for cold climates, as the air-cooled engine eliminated the need for a water pump, hoses and anti-freeze.

The Franklin was America's most successful air-cooled automobile during the early 20th Century. It was also one of the most elegant cars of its time, as well as technically innovative for its shock-absorbing wooden frame and full-elliptic leaf springs. The suspension and lightweight construction resulted in an exceptionally smooth, comfortable ride and greatly reduced tire wear.

Because air-cooled Franklins needed no radiator, they wore a series of unusual hood styles. The long "barrel hood" design seen on this car was used from 1905 to 1910 to house a longitudinally mounted engine. The 1907 Type D Franklins were powered by an overhead-valve four that displaced 227 cubic inches. In addition to the intake and exhaust valves in the head, however, each cylinder had a second exhaust valve at the bottom of the piston stroke. Having pioneered this feature, the H. H. Franklin Manufacturing Company claimed these auxiliary exhaust ports released most of the burned gas and excess heat.

The elegant 1907 Type D Landaulet was priced at $4,000, and this is the last-surviving one known. The stylish rear compartment features plush seating, upholstered doors, silk curtains, a card case and speaker tube to communicate with the driver. The mahogany-framed front windshield slides up under the ceiling and the rear roof section can be folded down for open-air riding.

1907 FRANKLIN

1907 WHITE STEAMER

Model G Touring

A 30-horsepower White steamer similar to this one was the third car in Fairbanks, arriving by sternwheeler in the fall of 1908. Imagine the interest the giant steamer generated when transporting passengers between Fairbanks and the mining town of Fox!

The White Sewing Machine Company added steam cars to its production line in 1900. High-quality automobiles, White steamers excelled in hill climbs, races and reliability runs. They were much more sophisticated than Stanley steamers and actually outsold the latter through 1910. That year, the company began manufacturing internal-combustion autos and in 1911 ceased production of steam cars.

White steamers had a semi-flash boiler consisting of a series of steel coils. Water was pumped into the top coil and then flashed into steam as it was forced though the coils below. The steam was then superheated in the lower coils before being routed to the two-cylinder compound engine. From 1902, Whites also used a condenser that captured the exhaust steam and returned it to the boiler. The condenser, which sat in front like an internal-combustion automobile's radiator, allowed the car to go farther on a tank of water than a non-condensing steam car (such as a pre-1915 Stanley).

White steamers were part of the White House's first official automobile fleet, while Model Gs were the very first cars purchased by the U.S. military. White steamers were also among the first automobiles transported to Alaska, where the big machines were put to work as passenger stages in Fairbanks and

Valdez. Only five Model Gs are known to still exist—and this one is unique among them for its short-coupled touring body which was custom-built by The Limousine Carriage Mfg. Co. of Chicago.

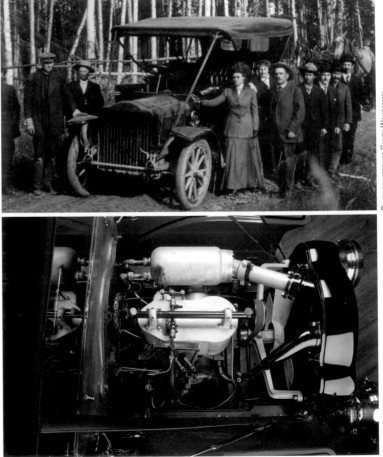

1907 WHITE STEAMER

1908 RAMBLER

1908 RAMBLER

Model 31 Five-Passenger Touring

After letting the block freeze with less than 1,000 miles on the engine, this Rambler's original owner put it in storage, where it sat for 67 years. It is in all-original condition except for the paint and rubber products.

Bicycle-maker Thomas Jeffrey was among the first Americans to become interested in automobiles, building his first one in 1897 and moving into production in 1902. Jeffrey quickly gained a reputation for building high-quality, medium-priced automobiles and became the second manufacturer after Oldsmobile to build cars on an assembly line.

The Rambler Model 31 was advertised as "the car for country roads." This touring car's most notable feature is its hinged body, which can be swung upward with ease to expose the two-cylinder, 206-cubic-inch engine and two-speed transmission. The tonneau can also be removed completely. The Jeffrey Company claimed a person could convert this "utility car" from a five-passenger touring car into a two-passenger roadster or flatbed truck in three to five minutes.

The last two-cylinder Ramblers were made in 1909. Thomas Jeffrey died suddenly the following April. His son Charles took control of the company and, in 1914, launched an all-new car, called the Jeffrey. Two years later, badly shaken after surviving the sinking of the *Lusitania*, Charles Jeffrey sold his company to ex-GM President Charles W. Nash—whose successor, George Mason, would revive the Rambler name for a new compact car in mid-1950.

1909 HUDSON

Model 20 Open Roadster

Built in late 1909, this is the oldest known all-original, unrestored Hudson.

Hudson's very first car, the Model 20, was a sporty little four-cylinder roadster advertised as "Strong – Speedy – Roomy – Stylish." It was attractively priced at $900, which was considered low for such a high-grade machine. The seat was positioned just ahead of the rear wheels and buyers had the option of choosing a rumble seat or a circular 25-gallon gas tank at the rear.

Although production began in 1909, the Hudson 20 was introduced as a 1910 model. It was an instant success, even giving the Model T Ford a run for its money. By July of 1910 Hudson had sold more than 4,000 Model 20s, a record for first-year sales among the fledgling auto industry. Later, Hudson became one of the first automakers to emphasize relatively inexpensive "closed" cars to protect riders from the elements—which further boosted sales.

The Fountainhead Museum has maintained this Hudson in original condition to preserve a living example of this model's history. While the car could be restored to show-quality condition, it would lose some of its historical significance. Modern materials, reproduced parts or parts substituted from similar models cannot accurately duplicate a car's original features. As the saying goes, "A car can only be original once."

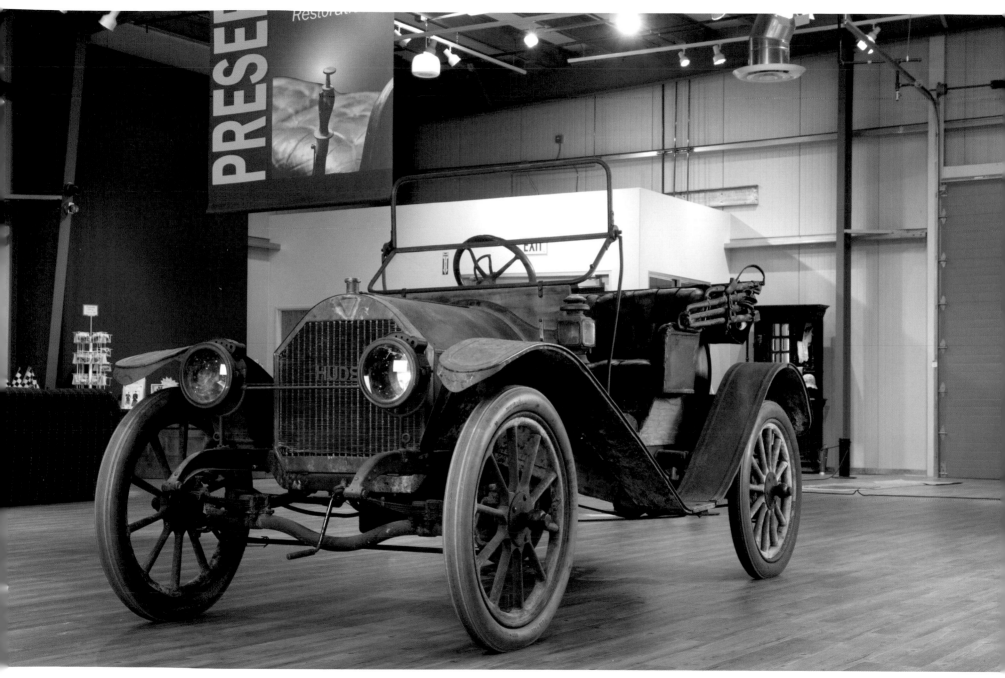

1909 HUDSON

1909 INTERNATIONAL

Model D Auto Buggy

The high wheeler was the first truly American car design that wasn't borrowed from Europe.

Briefly popular around the same time that Henry Ford launched his Model T, "high wheelers" were characterized by their mechanical simplicity and tall, wooden-spoke wheels with solid rubber tires. The International Harvester Company (IHC) Auto Buggy is a fine example: essentially a modified horse-drawn wagon equipped with an air-cooled, two-cylinder engine and two-speed transmission. The International has been cited as the most rugged of the roughly 280 makes of high wheelers built in America.

High wheelers were especially popular among farmers. They were easy to repair and better at negotiating muddy and rutted country roads that often clogged the smaller wheels of conventional cars. The wheels on this Model D are set 60 inches apart to fit in the tracks made by wagons of its day.

International promoted the Auto Buggy as a superior alternative to horses, stating, "This auto does not shy, balk or run away." A removable rear seat and sideboards allowed farmers to use the vehicle as a light truck during the week and as a family car on Sundays.

1909 INTERNATIONAL

1909 OLDSMOBILE

Model D Palace Touring

The Olds Palace Touring was one of the first touring cars to offer some enclosure for the driver and front-seat passenger, even though the small "demi-doors" didn't enclose much!

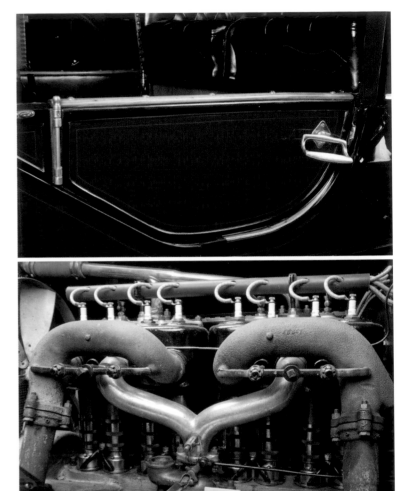

Ransom Eli Olds was a giant in the early American automobile industry. Although he left the Olds Motor Works in 1904 and began production of Reo automobiles, the Oldsmobile marque lasted until 2004—and then closed its doors as the oldest-surviving U.S. automaker.

The new, four-cylinder Palace Touring models introduced in 1906 were considerably larger and more luxurious than any of Olds' earlier productions. Although initial sales of the big Oldsmobiles were slow, many credit the Fours produced from 1906-1911 with the long-term success of Olds Motor Works. In

1908 Oldsmobile became a division of General Motors Corporation and in 1909 achieved its highest production to date.

This rare Model D has an inline four-cylinder, 336-cubic-inch engine that generates 40 hp. It covered 2,000 tour miles just prior to being acquired by the Fountainhead Museum.

1909 OLDSMOBILE

1909 STANLEY

Model R Roadster

Renowned for their tremendous acceleration and power, Stanley Steamers could go as fast backwards as forward.

In 1897 twin brothers Francis E. and Freelan O. Stanley produced the first example of what would become the best-known steam car in the world. After a brief stint with Locomobile, the twins re-opened their own steam-car business in 1901 and quickly gained a reputation for breathtaking performance. In 1906, a Stanley racer set a world land speed record of 127.6 mph that would stand for five years.

Compared to an internal-combustion car, a Stanley was easy to drive, quiet and odorless. A simple touch of the throttle lever set it in motion, and there were no gears to change. On the other hand, it takes about 40 minutes to fire up this Model R from cold to an operating pressure of 450-500 psig. Although many people are nervous about riding in an auto with a boiler full of live steam, there has never been a documented case of a Stanley exploding while in use. The boilers are fitted with safety valves, and if those fail, excessive pressure will rupture a joint and extinguish the burner before the boiler can burst.

The 20-hp "R" is today considered one of the most desirable Stanleys—sturdier than the Model H it replaced, yet lighter than the Model 71 that replaced it; and more nimble than Stanley's bigger 30-hp models while more powerful than the 10-hp cars. Nearly

11,000 Stanley steamers were produced, and today there are more Stanleys preserved, restored and operating than any other steam car. However, very few Model Rs are known to exist.

1909 STANLEY

1911 OAKLAND

1911 OAKLAND

Model 24 Roadster

From 1908 to 1910, Oaklands won more notable hill climbs than any other car.

Edward Murphy, founder of the Pontiac Buggy Company, and Alanson Brush, who had designed the early Cadillacs and would later build Brush automobiles, launched the Oakland Motor Car Company in 1907. In April of 1909 Oakland officially became a holding of General Motors, and with a new all-four-cylinder lineup sales increased dramatically. This success established Oakland as a viable competitor in the rapidly growing automobile market.

Oakland was known for producing stylish and powerful cars. The attractive Model 24 was introduced in 1910 as a two-passenger runabout equipped with a four-cylinder L-head engine and three-speed transmission. While not as powerful as Oakland's larger models, it performed exceptionally well in races and hill climbs.

Advertised as "The Car with a Conscience," Oakland production reached 3,386 cars in 1911, and by 1912 Oakland was the eighth largest American car manufacturer. In 1926, Oakland introduced the lower-priced Pontiac line—and then faded into the shadow of its own offspring's success.

1912 PEERLESS

1912 PEERLESS

Model 36-K Seven–Passenger Touring

Originally a manufacturer of clothes wringers, Peerless became one of the most highly respected luxury carmakers of the early 20th Century.

The Peerless Motor Car Company was known for innovation, having very early on offered an accelerator pedal, hinged steering wheel and a front-mounted engine with direct shaft drive to the rear axle. Peerless was also among the first carmakers in the U.S. to develop a production six-cylinder engine.

The marque's grandiose slogan, "Peerless—All That The Name Implies," was appropriate for such a high-quality and stylish automobile. In 1912 Peerless offered five models, each of which could be customized to suit an individual buyer's tastes. Wealthy patrons paid $5,000 for a Model 36 Touring, a massive car that rode on a 137-inch wheelbase and stood over seven feet tall. A 577.5-cubic-inch T-head six with its inline cylinders cast in pairs powered the car.

This beautiful, Brass Era car exemplifies why Peerless was included with Packard and Pierce-Arrow in the "Three P's" of early motoring royalty. Of the 450 Model 36s produced, only a handful are known to still exist, likely because their cast-aluminum bodies commanded high prices during wartime scrap drives. A victim of the Great Depression, the Peerless Company ended car production in 1932 and turned to making beer, becoming quite successful as Carling Breweries.

1912 PREMIER

Series N Model 6-60 Roadster

This Premier is one of the largest Brass Era roadsters ever built.

Premier automobiles were known for their powerful engines, attractive lines and superb performance. Premier was one of the first companies to use a vertical motor with the cylinders cast in pairs and overhead valves placed on opposite sides of the head. The Premier Motor Manufacturing Company claimed that the oak leaf on their 1903 radiator badge was the first use of an emblem as an automobile trademark.

In 1910 Premier introduced their six-cylinder Model 6-60, an attractive and imposing car. The 1912 version rode on a 140-inch wheelbase and was powered by a 501-cubic-inch T-head engine that generated 60 hp. The Fountainhead Museum's Premier was part of the Nethercutt Collection from 1964 to 2010. Former owner J. B. Nethercutt claimed the car had "a lot of go, and almost no whoa!"

This award-winning Premier has a unique air starter. Before stopping the car, the driver turns on an air pump to build up 150 psi in a tank. To re-start the car, the driver opens a valve and air is distributed via copper pipes to each cylinder in proper firing order. The air, instead of combustion, forces

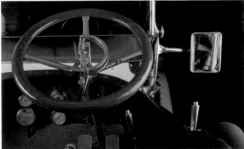

each piston down and the car starts with virtually no noise.

1912 PREMIER

1913-14 RAUCH & LANG

Electric Brougham

This Cinderella coach is essentially a drawing room on wheels.

Electric-powered cars were all the rage in the early 1900s, with Rauch & Langs among the most prestigious. Electric cars especially appealed to wealthy, urban women for their simplicity, quiet operation and elegance. The stylish Rauch & Lang brougham was designed for conversation, with the front passengers facing the driver's seat in the rear. The tall coach provided ample headroom for the fashionably large hats of the day, while the crystal vase mounted on one roof pillar could be filled with fresh flowers daily.

Although many automobiles began offering steering wheels in 1901, electric cars retained tiller bars, hinged to provide access to the driver's seat. Since it lacks an internal combustion engine, there was no need for a radiator. Two forty-volt batteries under the hood were wired in series to provide 80 volts to the motor. Under ideal conditions, the car could travel 70 miles on one charge.

This Rauch & Lang's history can be traced to 1934, when the Princeton Auto Museum acquired it from the original owner. Although that museum presented it as a 1912 model, our research indicates it was likely manufactured in 1913 or 1914. Regardless of its age, it is a rare gem that has survived in its original condition, with the exception of a new paint job in the 1950s and new tires and batteries.

1913-14 RAUCH & LANG

3. THE NICKEL ERA

1913–1929

Named for the use of nickel plating on cars, the Nickel Era saw a tremendous rise in the popularity of the automobile. Henry Ford kicked off the era with the launch of the moving assembly line, allowing him to continually decrease the price of the wildly popular Model T. New automakers proliferated, including Dodge, Willys-Knight, Chrysler and Pontiac. The development of Duco quick-drying lacquer in 1924 further ushered in the era of mass auto production.

This era brought many technical advances, including four-wheel brakes, hydraulic braking systems and the first modern power-assisted brakes; plus safety glass, all-steel bodies and, in 1929, the first easy-shifting Synchromesh transmission. Open cars gave way to closed-body sedans as the vehicle of choice for families. The spirit of the Roaring Twenties was personified by the increased demand for fast cars and custom-designed luxury models.

During this period Alaska experienced a surge in the automobile passenger stage business after Bobby Sheldon drove the first car over the Valdez-Fairbanks Trail in 1913. For years, Fairbanks residents could read about stage arrivals and new car purchases in the "Gasoline Dope" section of the local newspaper. By 1924 there were 1,225 cars in Alaska, including models by Ford, Overland, Reo, King, Cadillac, Packard, Dodge and Studebaker.

Chiffon and silk day dresses; silk party dress with lace overlay (ca. 1925-29)

A Ford Model T gets some equine assistance on the road through the Chatanika Valley. Woodrow Johnson Papers 2007-64-657; Archives, University of Alaska Fairbanks

1914 MOLINE-KNIGHT

Model MK-50 Touring

In a 1913 test, a Moline-Knight sleeve-valve motor ran a remarkable 337 hours non-stop at wide-open throttle without any adjustments, setting a world endurance record. The company claimed the test demonstrated the "incomparable superiority" of the Moline-Knight over conventional poppet-valve engines, and led them to advertise their car as the "Wrecker of World's Records."

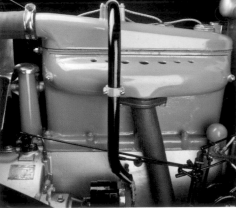

The Moline Automobile Company caused quite a stir in 1914 when it announced that its new models would feature smooth-running Knight sleeve-valve engines. As required by the standard licensing arrangement with inventor Charles Yale Knight, Moline cars would subsequently be called Moline-Knights. Moline's claims for the Knight engine included more power, efficiency, flexibility and durability than could be achieved with conventional poppet valves. It was also remarkably quiet. And at least initially, the high-quality Moline-Knight was less expensive than other Knight-engined cars as well.

Apparently the Moline-Knight was a personable car, being advertised as "cheerful, willing and fearless of distance and hills." Sir Galahad, "the most perfect of King Arthur's Knights of the Round Table," adorned the radiator emblem. In 1914 Moline-Knight offered this five-passenger touring model with room for two auxiliary seats. Only 11 Moline-Knights, including three 1914 Model MK-50s, are known to still exist.

1914 MOLINE-KNIGHT

1914 WOODS MOBILETTE

1914 WOODS MOBILETTE

Model 3 Tandem Roadster Cyclecar

Brakes were optional for an additional $10.

The Woods Mobilette was advertised as America's first "cyclecar"—a lightweight, chain-drive automobile that was little more than a motorcycle with four wheels. In the U.S., a cyclecar was defined as a vehicle with four wheels, a narrow tread and an engine displacement no greater than 71 cubic inches. Cyclecars had fewer features than typical autos of the day, but served as very inexpensive and efficient alternatives. Of the more than 240 companies that produced cyclecars from 1913-1916, the Woods Mobilette Company was one of the most successful.

This 450-lb Woods Mobilette roadster carried two people, with the passenger seated directly behind the driver. The car's design was narrow and lightweight, which offered excellent maneuverability, but its low clearance and 36-inch tread restricted it to city driving. The 12-hp, four-cylinder engine could power the little car to a top speed of 35 mph. Its reported fuel economy of 35-40 mpg would be the envy of many of today's drivers.

The Woods Mobilette sold for $380; optional equipment included speedometer ($11), windshield ($15), top ($15) and, according to at least one source, brakes ($10). Although inexpensive, it couldn't compete for comfort and reliability with Ford's Model T—which, by 1916, sold for just $10 more.

1917 OWEN MAGNETIC

1917 OWEN MAGNETIC

Model M-25 Touring

The Owen Magnetic was one of the most expensive U.S. automobiles produced at a time when the average car cost about $1,000 and a Ford Model T cost under $400.

The Owen Magnetic, advertised as "The Car of a Thousand Speeds," was one of the most unusual and technologically advanced cars of its time. It had no gears to shift and no clutch or flywheel. Instead, its gasoline engine turned a generator that powered an electric motor that drove the rear axle.

The 1917 Model M-25 carried a 303-cubic-inch, six-cylinder L-head Buda engine. Its unique electric transmission, which Justin Entz designed in 1897, produced an unlimited number of forward speeds. Unfortunately, Owen Magnetics were difficult and expensive to maintain, while separate controls for the throttle and transmission speed could make one complicated to drive. These challenges, coupled with the car's high price of $3,150 to over $6,000, limited sales and led to the company's demise.

Still, the Owen Magnetic was a car ahead of its time and an excellent example of the ingenuity of early automakers. Celebrities, including Italian opera star Enrico Caruso, were drawn to the elegance and smooth operation of this "aristocrat of motor cars." Of the 974 Owen Magnetics built from 1915 to 1921, only about a dozen are known to survive. Why this one has a unique second brake pedal for the front passenger remains a mystery.

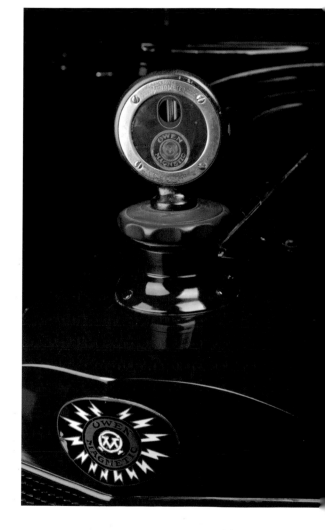

1917 FORD

Model T Snow Flyer

Man flew before he developed a motorized vehicle that could travel on snow.

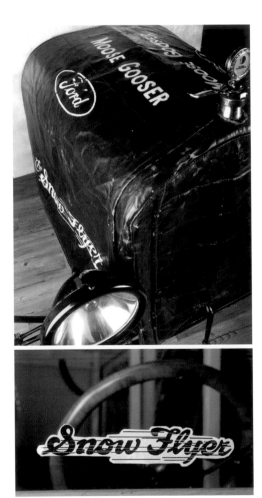

In 1913, Virgil White of New Hampshire put wooden runners on the front of a Ford Model T and added tractor treads on tandem rear wheels. He patented his "Snowmobile" kit—the first recorded use of the term—in 1917, more than 35 years before the first modern day recreational snowmobile appeared.

The Snow Flyer was a competitor to White's Model T Snowmobile. Both were used primarily for business—by mail carriers, country doctors, loggers, utility companies and farmers. This one was built on a 1917 Ford Model T chassis and carries a beautiful depot hack body made from ash. Its front wheels have been relocated to a dummy axle ahead of the rear wheels, which drive the continuous metal tracks. It has a high compression head and Hall-Scott rear end with a 10-tooth pinion to help it power over big snowdrifts.

This Snow Flyer was featured in the documentary film *The Incredible Model T Snowmobile Rediscovered*, and is a popular attraction at Fairbanks' annual Tired Iron vintage snowmobile rally.

1917 FORD

1917 PIERCE-ARROW

1917 PIERCE-ARROW

Model 66-A Seven-Passenger Touring

Because its massive engine had so much power and torque, the Model 66 was ranked among the mightiest automobiles of its era.

Built by a company that originally manufactured birdcages, iceboxes and bicycles, the Pierce-Arrow was one of America's most prestigious luxury automobiles. As one of the legendary "Three P's" of automotive royalty alongside Packard and Peerless, Pierce-Arrow was renown for quality, reliability and magnificent performance.

The Pierce-Arrow Motor Car Company produced the Model 66 from 1910 to 1918. The pinnacle of the series, the extraordinary Model 66-A introduced in 1913, was a car of staggering proportions, power and elegance. Towering more than seven feet tall and riding on a 147-1/2-inch wheelbase, the touring car's fine quality, smooth performance and regal coachwork allowed seven passengers to travel in high style and comfort. The cast aluminum body was lightweight and rigid, which reduced vibration, buckling and warping.

The Model 66-A carried one of the largest production engines ever to power an American passenger car. At 825 cubic inches, the big side-valve six was more than twice the size of most of its competitors. Not surprisingly, the Model 66 had poor fuel efficiency (8.5 mpg), but this was offset by a 36-gallon fuel tank that allowed the 5,250-lb leviathan to travel 300 miles on one fill.

Only 14 Model 66s—seven of them from 1917—are known to still exist. This particular

Model 66-A is a car of great provenance and is considered by many Pierce-Arrow enthusiasts to be the finest example of its model in the world. It has won numerous awards, including two First in Class honors at the Pebble Beach Concours d'Elegance.

1918 STUTZ

Series S 4-passenger Bulldog Special

The Bulldog is essentially a Stutz Bearcat with seating for four.

Although not as famous as its legendary predecessor, the stylish Bulldog Special introduced in 1915 was identical to the Stutz Bearcat except that it carried a four-passenger sport touring body. The Stutz Company's goal was to continue the sporty image and exceptional performance of the Bearcat while providing more room and comfort for passengers.

Late in 1917, all Stutz models switched from engines supplied by the Wisconsin Motor Manufacturing Co. to Stutz's own four-cylinder T-head with four valves per cylinder. Although the Bulldog was still heavier than the Bearcat and was equipped with a windshield and folding top, it could attain a respectable speed of 75 mph.

By then Bulldogs came in four- and six-passenger body styles, with the former priced at $2,650. The hood and cowl had been redesigned to blend better with the body lines, and instrument boards were added for the first time.

Despite its superb performance with practicality, the Bulldog never acquired the cachet of the Bearcat. Roughly 1,800 Stutz automobiles of all models were produced in 1918 and only a mere handful survive, including this unrestored example.

1918 STUTZ

1919 STUDEBAKER

Series 19 Model EG "Big Six" Manley Wrecker

The Sixes were the cars that would eventually make Studebaker famous.

collaborations with Garford and the Everitt-Metzger-Flanders Company under their belts, Studebaker finally began manufacturing their first complete, internal-combustion cars in 1913. These included their first Sixes, which, along with Premier, were the first mass-production cars to have six-cylinders cast en bloc.

Like the first tow truck invented in 1915, all wreckers of the era were created by converting a sturdy automobile into a truck. The Studebaker Big Six certainly qualified as sturdy: its 354-cubic-inch L-head engine developed 60 hp and more than enough torque to tow a broken-down Reo or Ford. This truck started life as a Studebaker four-door, seven-passenger touring car, the only Big Six body style offered in 1919. Its original owner converted it to wrecker in 1926.

Manley Manufacturing Company of York, Pennsylvania made the towing mechanism on this wrecker. They claimed theirs was the first automobile wrecking crane manufactured for dealers and garage owners. The crane's swivel-nose mechanism allowed disabled vehicles to be pulled directly from any angle. A towing saddle developed by Manley distributed the weight of the vehicle being towed over the full width of the tow truck's frame, even though the crane's base was relatively small.

After making their fortune supplying wagons during the Civil War and Westward Expansion Movement, the Studebaker Brothers entered the car market in 1902. With a decade of electric car production and brief, internal-combustion

1919 STUDEBAKER

1920 ARGONNE

Model D 2-Passenger Roadster

Flashy styling backed by proven components from reputable suppliers formed a popular formula for success in the 1920s. But few such "assembled" cars were flashier than the dramatically named Argonne.

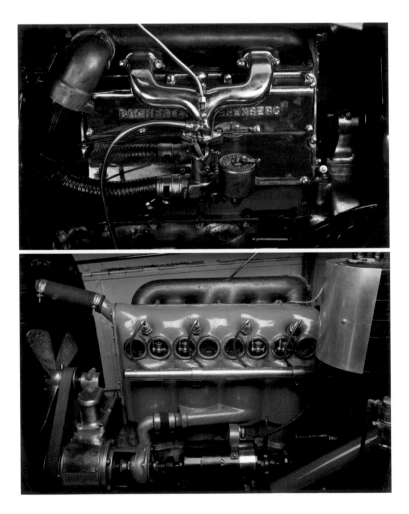

Fresh from his work for the similarly conceived Biddle, designer Otto R. Bieler debuted the Argonne—named for the marathon Great War battle—in January 1920. Dramatically low, lacking running boards and sporting a pointed radiator and tire-hugging fenders, the Argonne was built in Jersey City but could easily have been mistaken for a custom European exotic.

Unfortunately, Bieler died after only a handful of Argonnes were built. His successor, Charles Singer, decided to switch from the Buda engine Argonne was using to a more powerful Duesenberg unit.

This was Duesenberg's remarkable "walking beam" engine, in which overhead, horizontal valves were operated directly from the camshaft via foot-long, vertical rocker arms pivoted on the right side of the block. To contemporary observers, these oversized rockers suggested the dramatic "walking beams" that teetered atop giant industrial engines. A 10th-place finish at Indianapolis in 1914, followed by 5th and 8th in 1915, helped secure the walking-beam Duesy's legendary status. In 1919, when Duesenberg moved on to an overhead-cam eight, the manufacturing rights to the walking-beam four were sold to Rochester Motors Corp. of Rochester, New York.

The Rochester-Duesenberg Model G-1 four powering this Argonne displaces 340 cubic inches and develops 81 hp at 2600 rpm—far more than the 50-hp L-head Buda, and requiring a major redesign of the chassis. Supplier contracts were cancelled, and the resulting lawsuits left Argonne bankrupt. Of the 24 Argonnes built, only the last two had the Duesenberg engine.

This is the last surviving Argonne with either engine. For many *(Continued on page 66)*

1920 ARGONNE

1920 ARGONNE

(Continued from page 64) years it was thought to be a Biddle before careful research by the Harrah's Automobile Collection revealed its true identity.

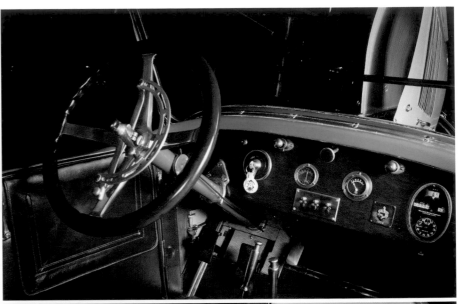

1921 HEINE-VELOX

V-12 Sporting Victoria

The Heine-Velox was the world's most expensive car of its time. Its $25,000 price tag was the equivalent of nearly $300,000 in today's dollars.

The Heine-Velox was one of the most interesting and unusual cars produced in the western United States. After the Great San Francisco Earthquake and subsequent fire destroyed the newly established Heine-Velox auto plant in 1906, Gustav Heine set aside his auto interests and rebuilt his successful piano manufacturing business. He never lost his desire for building cars, though, and in 1918 he announced he would build "the most expensive automobile in America."

Heine's enormous, curious-looking automobiles carried features that were big advances in 1921. Unlike the vertical windscreens on other cars, the Heine-Velox's was deeply sloped to reduce glare and was seated in rubber to stop squeaks and leaks. The headlamps perched on the fenders had both high and low beams. A Heine-Velox sedan was one of the first American cars to feature four-wheel hydraulic brakes.

Other innovations included a gravity oil-feed reserve tank that allowed the engine oil level to be maintained from the driver's seat, and a slanted dashboard designed to hide the gear shifter, hand brake and steering column (albeit not very successfully). A modified Weidely V-12 engine displacing 389.5 cubic inches and producing 115 hp could allegedly propel the massive car to a top speed of 75 mph.

Gustav Heine said, "When you ride in this car, you ride *in* it, not on top of it," because the body was mounted to the sides of the frame, instead of the top. This provided more structural rigidity and a lower center of gravity. Various racks, shelves and boxes could carry luggage at the front, rear or on either side of the car. Only four and one-half of these unique vehicles were ever built: *(Continued on page 68)*

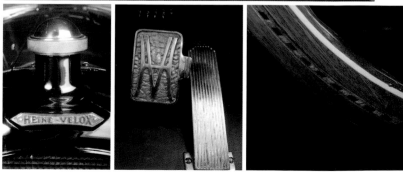

(Continued from page 67) three sedans, an unfinished limousine and this 4,500-lb Sporting Victoria. Only two complete cars survive. The Heine-Velox price tags of $17,000-$25,000 were shocking for the day, considering one could buy a Rolls Royce for $12,000 and a Ford Model T for less than $500. Heine never did sell any of his cars, but not because of the price. It seems he simply couldn't bear to part with them, even when a Hollywood movie star allegedly mailed the company a check for $25,000. In 1963 Heine's estate donated the Sporting Victoria to the Harrah collection in Reno, and the Fountainhead Museum acquired it in 2008.

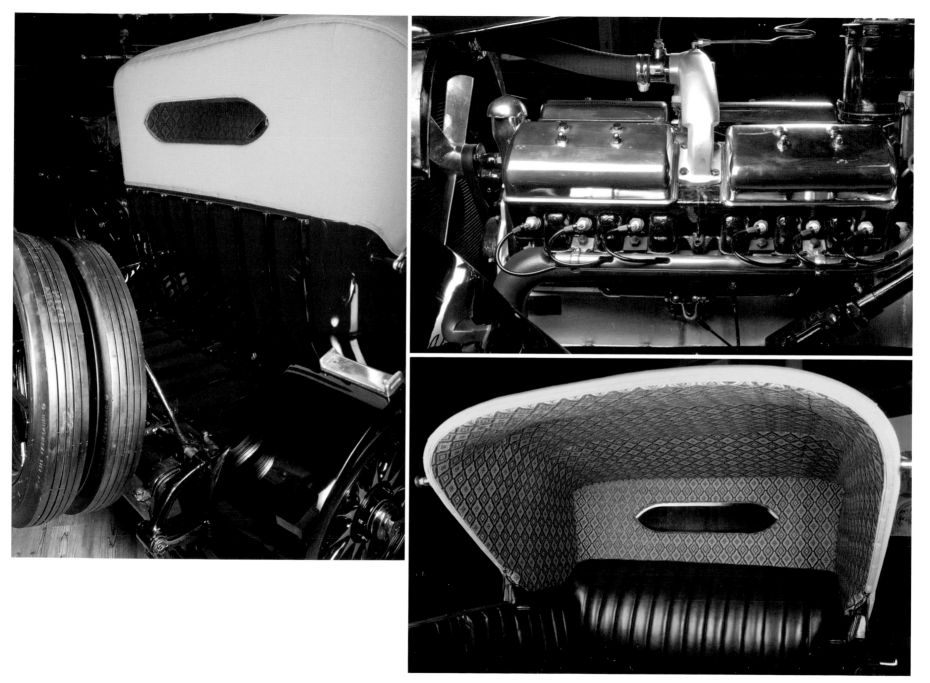

1921 DANIELS

1921 DANIELS

Model D Six-Passenger Touring

"The Distinguished Car to the Discriminating"

The Daniels was a low production, high-quality luxury car built from 1916–1924 in Reading, Pennsylvania. Company president George Daniels took great pride in his cars

and personally examined each one, sparing no expense if any detail needed to be redone. No two were alike, as each was built to suit a buyer's individual tastes.

The Daniels was a big and formidable automobile, with some models weighing three tons. Its "cathedral type" radiator shell and core were made from a single pewter casting. The Daniels was also powerful, carrying one of the first production V-8 engines when it debuted in 1916. Supplied by Herschel-Spillman, its cylinders were cast in blocks of four, bolted to an eight-quart crankcase. This engine was said to burn an average of one quart of oil every 200 miles.

Daniels production peaked in 1921 with the Model D, the company's last and finest model. Now powered by Daniels' own 404-cubic-inch L-head V-8, producing 90 hp at 2,000 rpm, it proved to be fast and very roadworthy. Company brochures promoted the Model D as "The Distinguished Car, with just a little more power than you'll ever need."

The Model D six-passenger touring car cost $5,350 at a time when one could buy a Ford Model T for $440. By then the Daniels Motor Car Company built most of the Model D bodies in their Reading factory, but this unrestored car features custom coachwork by Fleetwood. Of the 1,960 Daniels produced, less than 10 are known to survive.

1922 WILLS SAINTE CLAIRE

1922 WILLS SAINTE CLAIRE

Model A-68 5-Passenger Sedan

A car that was too well built to sell profitably at a reasonable price.

After Childe Harold Wills left his job as Ford Motor Company's chief designer and metallurgist in 1919, he used his sizeable share of Ford profits to begin production of one of America's best-engineered and most advanced luxury automobiles—the Wills Sainte Claire. It was a stylish and powerful car graced with a flying goose on the radiator emblem and cap.

Wills was famous for pioneering molybdenum steel in the auto industry, using the exceptionally strong alloy for every component of the car subjected to even minimal stress. His V-8, one of the first overhead-cam engines designed for passenger-car use, was partly inspired by the Hispano-Suiza aircraft engine of the recent war. Other advanced features included full-pressure lubrication, a water-jacketed intake manifold, a back-up light that switched on automatically in reverse gear, and both high and low-beam headlights.

Wills' perfectionism led to assembly line shutdowns each time he wanted to make an improvement. These delays drove up production costs and reportedly the company lost money on every car. Despite their high quality, and with prices ranging from $2,800-$4,700, Wills never sold enough cars to make a profit.

Of the 12,000 Wills Sainte Claires made, approximately 80 are known to survive.

1927 STUTZ

1927 STUTZ

Vertical Eight Custom Series AA Black Hawk Boattail Speedster

The dramatic Black Hawk speedster recalled the romance of the Bearcat in a new, more modern and more sophisticated Stutz.

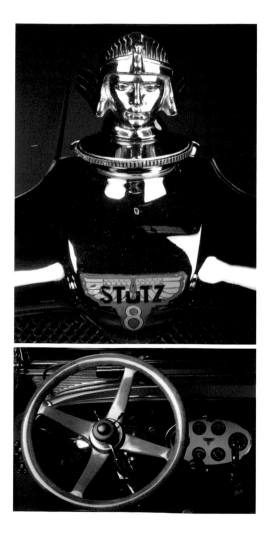

Stutz introduced their Vertical Eight in 1926. The new design marked a radical departure from the Stutz Motor Car Company's earlier cars and emphasized luxury, sophistication and safety over the popular Bearcat's rough, loud and fast image. Its "Safety" chassis employed a double-drop frame and worm-driven rear axle that made it possible for the body to sit quite low. This in turn dropped the center of gravity and reduced the danger of tipping. Other improved safety features included advanced four-wheel hydraulic brakes and wire-reinforced glass in the windshield and side windows.

The Series AA Stutz was powered by a single-overhead-cam straight-eight that, by 1927, displaced 299 cubic inches and delivered 95 hp. The Egyptian sun god, Ra, adorned the radiator. Egyptian ornamentation became the rage, even on clothing, following the discovery of King Tutankhamen's tomb in 1922.

All Stutz Vertical Eights were striking, but the (initially) limited-production Black Hawk Speedster was downright stunning, with tire-hugging fenders, a raked windshield, streamlined boattail, dual side-mounts and step plates instead of running boards. Packing modified "Challenger" engines, Stutz Black Hawks won every stock race they entered in 1927 to become that year's AAA Stock Car Champion. For 1928, the Challenger-powered

Black Hawk became a cataloged production model.

As with other desirable classics, many Black Hawks seen today are not originals, but instead carry period-correct reproduction bodies. This car, originally a Series AA coupe, was re-bodied as a speedster in the 1970s. While not original, the impeccably re-created coachwork captures the fabulous style that embodied the Roaring Twenties.

4. THE CLASSIC ERA

1930s

While the Classic Era actually spans 1925 to 1948, the 1930s automobiles in the Fountainhead Collection best represent the pinnacle of design, custom styling and engineering refinement that exemplified the era. These were the ultimate luxury cars designed for—and by—wealthy patrons, utilizing the artistic skills of such gifted stylists as Alan Leamy, Ray Dietrich and Raymond Loewy, and of storied coachbuilders like Fleetwood, Murphy and LeBaron.

These cars were all about lines—elegant, flowing contours that visually streamlined the body. Sleek profiles, long hoods, stylish radiators and skirted fenders were matched by sumptuously appointed interiors customized for the buyer. Even the tiny American Austin (far from being a luxury classic) sported stylish coachwork designed by Russian Count Alexis de Sakhnoffsky.

Most of these beauties were matched by unparalleled performance. Modern independent front suspension was introduced during this era, and engines were moved forward between the front wheels. These changes resulted in tremendous improvements in ride quality. Cadillac's revolutionary V-16 of 1930 sparked a "cylinder race" among luxury automakers, while solidifying Cadillac's reputation for engineering leadership.

Some 1930s luxury cars no doubt found their way to Alaska. However, stalwarts like Model A Fords were far more practical for the Territory's harsh road conditions and the work needs of the hardy souls carving out a living in the Last Frontier.

Chiffon day dress worn in 1930s Fairbanks.

On loan from *Pioneer Ladies Auxiliary Igloo 8*

Three ladies pose with a 1935 Chrysler Airflow near Worthington Glacier north of Valdez. Note the tractor treads on the rear tires. CROSSON FAMILY PAPERS 2006-103-128; ARCHIVES, UNIVERSITY OF ALASKA FAIRBANKS

1931 CORD

Series L-29 Cabriolet

America's first production front-wheel drive car was also a design masterpiece.

The Cord L-29 was famous for pairing revolutionary front-wheel drive with strikingly beautiful design. The chassis sat unusually low due to the absence of a conventional rear-wheel driveline, giving the car an elegant, racy look. Designer Alan Leamy further set off the Cord's low profile with gracefully curved fenders, a sharply veed grille, suicide doors, large running boards and gleaming brightwork. The split design of the bumper and oval cover over the transaxle assembly were designed to emphasize the unique front-drive unit.

The Cord's eight-cylinder inline L-head Lycoming engine displaced 298.6 cubic inches and developed 115 hp at 3,300 rpm. The clutch, three-speed transmission and differential sat directly in front of the engine in a 180-degree reversal from conventional cars.

Although the L-29's stunning good looks and rakish silhouette attracted celebrity buyers like Mary Pickford and the Marx Brothers, sales barely surpassed 5,000 during three years of production. Less than two months after the Cord's introduction, the stock market crashed and production of the L-29 ceased at the end of 1931.

The Cabriolet is one of the most sought-after body styles of the Cord L-29. This one has fewer than 14,000 original miles on it, is wonderfully preserved and still has its original top and interior.

1931 CORD

1932 CADILLAC

Series 452-B V-16 Imperial Limousine by Fleetwood

The car that launched—and won—
the multi-cylinder wars.

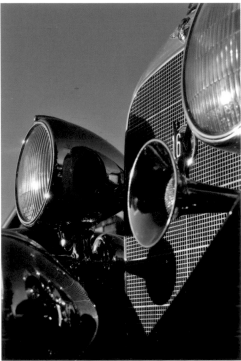

In 1930 Cadillac introduced the world's first production V-16 automobile engine. This revolutionary power plant not only set off a "cylinder race" among America's ultra-luxury automakers, it handily won it, and in the process firmly established Cadillac's reputation as an engineering giant among the world's most prestigious marques.

The Series 452 V-16 engine designed by Owen Nacker was not just an engineering masterpiece—it was also a work of art. It was engineered as two straight-eight overhead valve engines, each equipped with its own fuel and exhaust system, set at a 45-degree angle and sharing a common crankshaft. The beautifully detailed engine displaced 452 cubic inches, produced 165 hp and could propel the 6,200-lb limousine to a top speed of 90 mph.

One road tester said the engine was ". . . so smooth and quiet throughout its range as to make it seem incredible that the car is actually being propelled by exploding gases."

All Cadillac V-16s were custom built and elaborately finished. This award-winning limousine has original Fleetwood coachwork set off by white-wall tires, dual side-mount spares and Cadillac's elegant heron hood ornament. The richly appointed, unrestored interior is separated into a chauffeur compartment and "owner's drawing room" complete with a smoking kit, lady's vanity, headliner hat net, rollup window shades and floor heater.

Only 49 Cadillac V-16 limousines were made in 1932, and a mere handful survive.

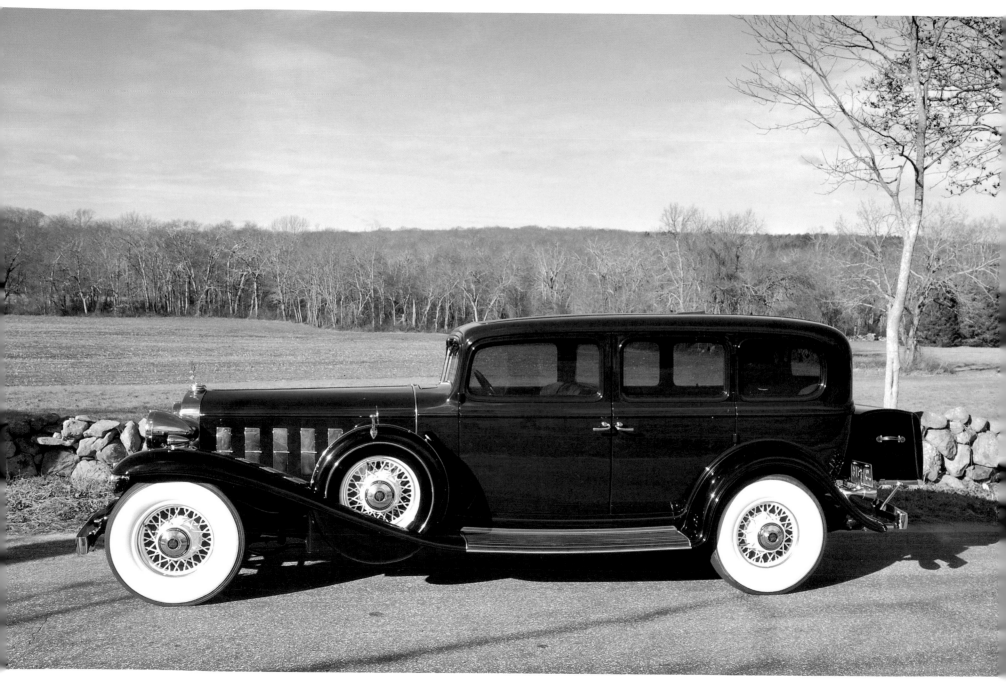

1932 CADILLAC

1932 CHRYSLER

Custom Imperial Series CL Convertible Sedan by LeBaron

The CL model is regarded by many collectors as the greatest of all Chryslers.

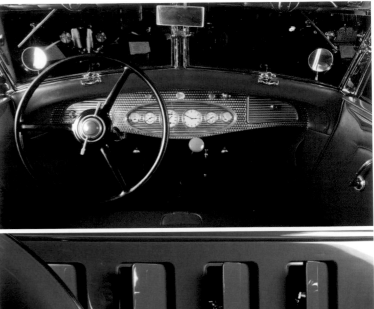

the most esteemed Imperials were the 1931-1933 models carrying semi-custom coachwork by LeBaron. The stylish design set off by the vee radiator, long hood and low, sweeping fenders was clearly inspired by the Cord L-29.

Sleek new bodies featured a distinctive "de Sakhnoffsky" engine hood that stretched all the way to the windshield, covering the traditional cowl. Only 49 CL convertible sedans were produced in 1932 and approximately 12 are known to survive. At $3,595, they were the most expensive semi-custom in the CL Series that year. Each carried an impressive, 385-cubic-inch straight-eight engine that developed 125 hp at 3,200 rpm with the standard "Silver Dome" cylinder head; or 135 hp with the optional, high-compression "Red Head." The 1932 Imperials also featured "Floating Power"—an innovative system that balanced the engine on two flexible rubber mountings and a single spring, thus isolating its noise and vibration from the chassis.

Each Chrysler Imperial CL was carefully crafted to the buyer's specifications. The LeBaron coachwork on this award-winning car includes hand-buffed leather seats, a leather dashboard with a machine-tooled instrument cluster and twin glove boxes, dual side-mounted spare tires, a curvy luggage trunk and a winged radiator cap graced with a bounding gazelle. Even the taillights are elegant!

The first Chrysler Imperials introduced for 1926 were designed to compete with Lincoln and Cadillac in the "affordable" luxury field. Renowned for their superior performance,

1932 CHRYSLER

1933 AUBURN

Model 12-161A Custom Boattail Speedster

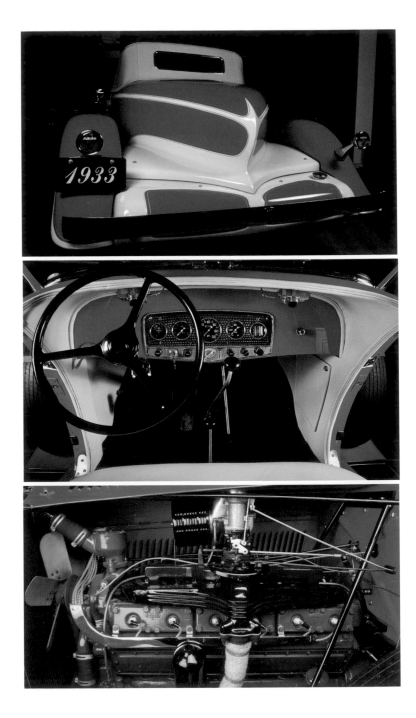

The wild and flashy design of this car is not just skin deep, for this was one of the fastest sports cars of its era.

powered American car and cost less than a third the price of a Packard Deluxe Eight.

With its rakish low profile and graceful lines, the Auburn boattail speedster became an immediate sensation following its introduction in 1928. An even more outrageous update for 1931—by Alan Leamy, designer of the Cord L-29 and Duesenberg Model J—kept the Speedster fresh in the public eye.

The V-12 was added to the line in 1932, and Auburn was soon ranked among the fastest sports cars of its era after breaking every stock car speed record for one to 500 miles that year. The 160-hp, 391-cubic-inch engine was very advanced for its day, utilizing a narrow, 45-degree vee and horizontal valves in unusual combustion chambers set at an angle to the cylinders.

V-12 Speedsters were catalogued in both mid-range "Custom" and maximum-deluxe "Salon" trim. According to the Auburn Cord Duesenberg Museum, only three boattail speedsters were produced in the Custom range in 1933, this being the last one built. Ironically, the beautiful Auburn's low cost likely contributed to its demise. A victim of "snob appeal," it was too inexpensive to appeal to the rich, and many assumed the car's quality was poor because the price was so low.

Auburn was the cornerstone of Errett Lobban Cord's automobile empire, which also included Cord and Duesenberg. Although very stylish and equipped with high-end features like Bijur lubrication, hydraulic four-wheel brakes and free wheeling, the Auburn was the most economical V-12-

1933 AUBURN

1933 HUPMOBILE

Silver Anniversary Series K-321 Victoria

The Hupmobiles of the early 1930s had the distinction of being the first automobiles styled by famed industrial designer Raymond Loewy.

Detroit-based Hupmobile reached its zenith in 1928, when the assembly of nearly 66,000 cars made it America's ninth-place automaker. When sales slipped the following year, Hupp Motor Car President DuBois "Pink" Young called in Raymond Loewy to re-style Hupp's premier eight-cylinder line.

The resulting Hupmobile eights, which debuted in January 1932, were downright stunning. Vertical-themed, vee-shaped radiator grilles loomed like mobile skyscrapers, capped by a fluted bauble and topped with a delicately dancing *H* inside a free-standing ring. Raked-

back windshields suggested speed, while providing the focal point for a sweeping belt molding that tapered dramatically to both front and rear. Most striking, though, were Loewy's new "cycle" fenders that tightly hugged the curves of the tires. Bucking the contemporary fashion for tapered fender "sweeps," they emphasized length by leaving more of the body side exposed.

Loewy stretched this theme even further for 1933. An even more massive radiator grille now leaned back at an angle like the windshield, flanked by deeper headlight buckets, and followed by an engine hood that flowed back over the cowl in the style usually attributed to Count Alexis de Sakhnoffsky. Adding to the Hupp's visual mass were new hood-side ventilation "doors," replacing 1932's slanted louvers. And Hupmobile sixes now enjoyed the same style, with the debut of the new Series K-32.

This 1933 K-321 Victoria is powered by a 228 cubic-inch L-head engine that develops 90 hp at 3,800 rpm. Hupp produced 7,318 of the Series K-321s in 1933, with the Victoria model selling for $1,060. Only seven 1933 K-321 Victorias are known to still exist.

1933 HUPMOBILE

1934 AMERICAN AUSTIN

1934 AMERICAN AUSTIN

Series 475 Standard Coupe

"Baby Austins" were popular among celebrities, including Al Jolson, W.C. Fields, Buster Keaton, Ernest Hemingway and the "Our Gang" kids. An American Austin was even featured in one of the earliest Mickey Mouse cartoons.

This diminutive automobile is the Americanized version of the British Austin Seven, which took Europe by storm in the 1920s. Like the cyclecar manufacturers of the teens, the promoters of the American Austin hoped to open up a market for small cars in the U.S. At only 105 inches long, these whimsical cars were 16 inches narrower and 28 inches shorter than any other car made in the U.S.

The American Austin was introduced in 1930 and, by 1932, buyers could choose among coupe, roadster and cabriolet models.

All were powered by a four-cylinder, 15-hp engine that displaced only 45.6 cubic inches. Advertisements boasted a top speed of 55 mph and guaranteed a fuel economy of 40 mpg.

Unfortunately, American Austins were never really taken seriously and were often the subject of jokes and college pranks. It didn't help that a larger Ford Model A cost less than American Austin's initially announced price of $445 (although that figure came down later), and that larger second-hand cars often appealed as better bargains.

For 1934, a Series 475 Standard Coupe listed for just $345, but by then the company was already in receivership. Still, American Austin dealer Roy Evans was able to reorganize the operation as American Bantam, and built a sleeker, sturdier version of the little Austin from 1937 through 1941.

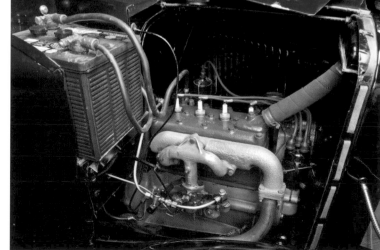

1936 PACKARD

7-Passenger 1408 Dual Windshield Touring

Many consider the Twelves of the 1930s to be the finest automobiles produced by the Packard Motor Car Company.

O ne of the "Three P's" of American motoring royalty, Packard introduced America's first production twelve-cylinder car in 1916. After discontinuing their Twin Six in 1923 to focus on straight eights, Packard wouldn't produce another twelve-cylinder engine until 1932—the same year that Lincoln, Pierce-Arrow and Auburn also released V-12s, all to rival the polycylindric Cadillac V-12 and V-16. Packard's side-valve V-12 nearly equaled the Cadillac overhead-valve V-16 in horsepower (160 vs. 165), and rivaled it for torque (322 lb-ft, vs. approximately 324).

By 1936 the whisper-quiet Packard V-12 displaced 473 cubic inches and developed 175 hp. Sporting semi-custom "Dietrich" coachwork—designed and crafted, in fact, in Packard's own custom shop—the Series 1408 Packards coupled superior performance with striking elegance. The elongated hood, central-hinged doors, bullet headlights and pontoon fenders helped place these Packards among the most desirable cars of the era

Still, 1936 was a pivotal year for Packard. In 1935, the company's first true mass-production model, the One-Twenty, had introduced Packard style and quality to the Buick price range. Its runaway success would guarantee Packard's survival through the Depression, but it also reduced the hand-built "Senior" Packards to corporate status symbols that contributed relatively little to the bottom line. Nineteen thirty-six would be the last full year for the touring body style, and the Senior Packards would not return after the war.

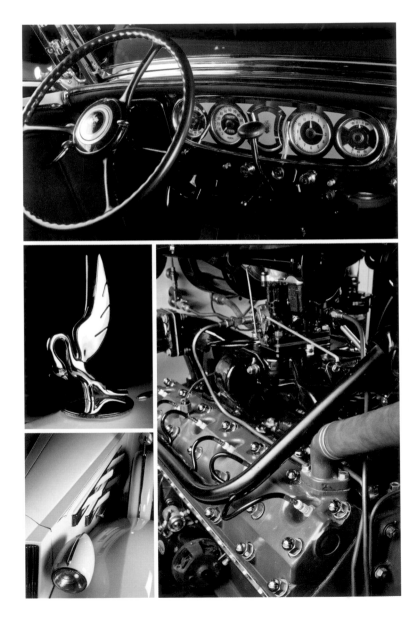

1936 PACKARD

5. MIDGET RACERS

In the grip of the Great Depression millions of Americans got caught up in a new brand of racing known as the Midgets. These small racecars typically weighed less than 900 lbs and enjoyed plenty of power, initially from highly modified four-cylinder passenger-car engines and later from thoroughbred racing units. Bodies and chassis were usually pieced together from parts found in junkyards, so no two cars were the same.

Midget racing grew in popularity like nothing else in the history of sports. By the mid-1930s nearly every horse track, speedway and many ballparks and fairgrounds saw the little cars chasing one another. Crowds loved the close, ferocious style of racing where drivers jockeyed for position and skidded around curves—occasionally on just one rear tire. Midgets powered by marine outboards— smoking and howling—added to the fun. Not surprisingly, the high power and small size of the cars combined to make Midget racing very dangerous, and a number of drivers were killed. Racecars of that era had no seatbelts or roll bars, and the drivers often wore only simple cloth helmets for head protection.

Midget racing reached Fairbanks in the late 1940s. Most races took place at the Rendezvous track north of town, but some were actually held on the ice of frozen rivers and lakes!

Bob Swanson in the #1 Wetteroth–Offenhauser midget racer, ca. 1935. FOUNTAINHEAD COLLECTION PHOTOGRAPH

1935 WETTEROTH-OFFENHAUSER

Midget Racer

During one competition in the late 1940s, the lone Offenhauser Midget was required to start half a lap behind the Ford and motorcycle-powered cars—but still won.

The potent 98-cubic-inch twin-cam Offenhauser was the first engine built specifically for Midget racing. Derived from the Miller straight-eight that had won the Indianapolis 500 in 1932, the four-cylinder "Offy" quickly outclassed the motley collection of modified passenger car, motorcycle and marine engines that had dominated the first Midget races. In fact, the Offy's performance so far surpassed that of other Midget engines that separate series were often held for them, while other times the number of Offys was limited in any one race.

It was promoter Earl Gilmore (of Gilmore Stadium) who first approached engine builder Fred Offenhauser in July 1934. The first two Offy midget engines were installed in chassis built by Louis Wetteroth. This is the *second* of those two cars. (Unfortunately, the Offy Midget engine in it now, while authentic, is not the original.) Driver Bob Swanson was unbeatable in it, winning the United Midget Association title in 1935. Swanson's exceptional driving skills and good looks attracted legions of fans. He went on to win many more Midget

races—and to finish sixth in the 1940 Indy 500—before being killed in a qualifier in 1940 at the age of 27.

Despite the advanced engine that motivated it, the chassis of Midget #1 is typical of its time—and rather unsophisticated by today's standards. Solid axles ride on parallel leaf springs up front and a transverse leaf spring in the rear, with Hartford friction shock absorbers all around.

1937 WINTERS-FORD V8-60

Midget Racer

Overheating was a major problem for the Ford V8-60 Midgets. They were known as "teakettles" and blew hoses regularly, sometimes terribly scalding their drivers.

This Ford-powered Midget (originally numbered S-41) was built by Stan Winters, who recruited Ralph Moody to drive it. Moody was "nearly unbeatable" in Midgets and later became a legendary stock car driver and mechanic. In 1956, he partnered with John Holman to become the most successful car-building team in motorsports history. The duo built virtually all of the factory Ford race cars from the '50s through the '70s—cars that were driven by such greats as Mario Andretti, A. J. Foyt, Parnelli Jones, Richard Petty, Jackie Stewart, Bobby Unser and Cale and Lee Roy Yarbrough.

Less costly than the thoroughbred Offy, the 136-cubic-inch "V8-60" debuted in Ford's 1937 passenger cars as a more economical alternative to the established 221-cubic-inch V-8. In stock tune it developed 60 hp—hence "V8-60"—vs. 85-90 hp for the big V-8. As a race engine the V8-60 proved fairly solid, and could be bored and stroked and hopped up with special cams, heads, manifolds and carburetors.

Other drivers of #41 included Don Hicks, Lane Murray, Andy Ellis, Art Sprague and Mel Wilbur. In 1948 Mel Wilbur crashed #41 during a race in Thompson, Connecticut.

1938 SOUTHWEST CHROME SPECIAL

Midget Racer

Outboard engine manufacturer Elto sold more Model 4-60 engines to Midget car racers than to boat racers, yet fewer than 12 Elto Midgets are known to still exist.

The Southwest Chrome Special—#35—was owned and driven on many California tracks by Ed "Elbows" Davis, who got his nickname from his unorthodox driving style that made him look like he was bulldogging a steer. It is powered by a water-cooled, four-cylinder, two-stroke horizontally opposed Elto outboard engine producing 85 hp at 8,500 rpm.

Of all the early home-built Midgets, none approached the success of those that were powered by outboard engines. This car is

typical, with its crankshaft standing vertically above a set of bevel gears that redirects the torque toward the rear wheels. Off the shelf, the 60-cubic-inch Elto boat-racing engine developed a remarkable one horsepower per each cubic inch. Aftermarket cylinder kits opened displacement up to 75 cubic inches and, by boosting the compression ratio to 10:1 and burning a mixture of 82 percent methanol, 10 percent benzol or toluene and 8 percent castor oil (for lubrication), one could push the power output even higher.

From 1936 through 1942, outboard-powered Midgets reigned supreme, consistently beating the even more powerful but heavier Offys. The Elto's light weight (just 91 lbs) and rapid acceleration made it particularly dominant on 1/5-mile board tracks—where, running wide-open, the two-stroke produced just enough torque to stick to the high banking. While these board tracks were popular with Midget racing fans, they were deadly to many unfortunate drivers.

1938 SOUTHWEST CHROME SPECIAL

Robert "Bobby" Sheldon and passengers in Fairbanks (ca. 1909). Photo courtesy of Frances Erickson

HISTORIC FASHION COLLECTION

Riding in early automobiles meant bumping and jouncing over dusty tracks, often faster than in a horse-drawn vehicle, but with no more protection from the elements. Along with the grit and mud of the roads, the relatively primitive engines often sputtered oil and smoke. Suddenly, people needed special goggles, coats and hats to

Day dress of silk brocade with tightly boned bodice and leg-of-mutton sleeves (ca. 1896)

Silk brocade bustle dress with tufted birds (ca. 1881-83). Detail at left.

Right: Silk and net evening gown with ethnic-inspired beading (ca. 1913-1917)

travel in any comfort. Thus began the parallel history of the automobile and modern fashion.

The Fountainhead Historic Fashion Collection is an eclectic mix of garments representative of the early years of auto history. It includes motoring clothes, everyday fashions and formal dress from the late Victorian period through the Swing era. In addition, select *(Continued on page 103)*

Two-piece silk jacquard visiting dress (ca. 1899-1904)

Edwardian wool walking suits (ca. 1910).

SUIT ON RIGHT ON LOAN FROM PIONEER LADIES AUXILIARY IGLOO 8

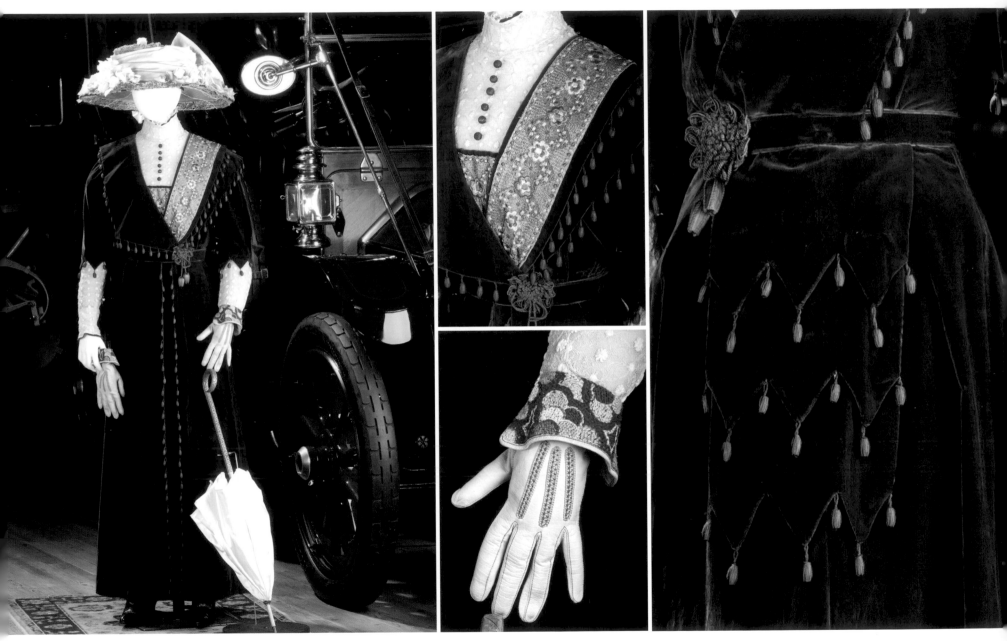

Titanic-era velvet street dress with elaborate

tassels and triangular edging (ca. 1912)

(Continued from page 101) garments from the 18th and pre-motoring 19th centuries provide a glimpse into the time before speed and streamlining became all the rage.

Displayed on life-size mannequins, the clothing is paired with automobiles of the appropriate age. The exhibits show how fashion changed from the Victorians' tightly corseted, restrictive clothing to the looser sophistication of Art Deco—just as automobiles evolved from boxy carriage shapes to sleek, stylized designs. *(Continued on page 104)*

Cashmere skating coat with fox collar (ca. 1905-1910) and 3-hide Alaska black bear coat (1915). BEAR COAT ON LOAN FROM ROCKY MACDONALD

Silk crepe opera gown with tunic overskirt and train (ca. 1911-1912)

HISTORIC FASHION COLLECTION

(Continued from page 103)

Alaskans tended to buy workhorse automobiles, but fashion was another matter. Our historic photograph displays and a special collection of clothing with Alaskan provenance illustrate that Alaskan women were just as interested in fashion as their sisters in the States. Women of means ordered dresses from San Francisco or Seattle; others employed local dressmakers. In spite of the often uncomfortable and primitive conditions,

Beaded Art Deco flapper dress attributed to Jean Patou (ca. 1925–1926)

Art Deco flapper coat of silk, lamé and gold metallic thread (ca. 1925–1929)

women dressed fashionably in white tea dresses and attended elegant balls with gentlemen in fine formal wear.

The museum's fashion collection includes hundreds of antique dresses, coats, hats, men's suits, shoes and accessories. Over 80 outfits are on display at any given time, helping to illustrate how America's love affair with the auto-mobile transformed everyday life and culture.

Dressing robe with tambour embroidery (ca. 1930s)

Evening gowns in satin, chiffon and lamé lace (ca. 1930–1934)

David Laiti's Pope-Toledo was the first car in Fairbanks, arriving by sternwheeler in August of 1908. MARY WHALEN COLLECTION 1975-84-464; ARCHIVES, UNIVERSITY OF ALASKA FAIRBANKS

Bobby Sheldon and his passengers ferried this Model T Ford across the Tanana River on two poling boats during their pioneering drive between Fairbanks and Valdez in 1913. Photo courtesy of Frances Erickson

ALASKA MOTORING HISTORY

"Go-Devil Appeared on the Streets Last Night for the First Time" proclaimed the *Fairbanks Weekly Times* on August 8, 1908. "The way some of the old sourdoughs rubber-necked when they saw the horseless carriage coming down Front Street would make a good picture for Puck's magazine. Somebody wanted to know if it burned wood or oil, while others guessed that it had to be wound up like an alarm clock."

Although Robert Sheldon's 1905 home-made runabout is heralded as Alaska's earliest car, the debut of the 50-hp Pope-Toledo noted above clearly indicated that the automobile had arrived for good in Fairbanks. It wouldn't take long for more

"road monsters" to make the sternwheeler journey up the Yukon and Tanana rivers, where they were quickly put into service ferrying passengers to the mining camps.

Initially, these "devil wagons" and "explosion carts" provided much excitement and entertainment. Most new owners had never driven a car before, accidents were frequent and some terrified passengers demanded to be let out after only a few miles. Extreme cold, deplorable road conditions and an absence of repair shops meant that Alaskan motorists required tremendous ingenuity and resourcefulness.

The Fountainhead Museum celebrates this rich motoring history by sharing the stories and hardships faced by Alaska's tenacious automotive pioneers. Many of the historic photographs decorating the museum's walls illustrate the north's unique motoring challenges, including the navigation of glacial streams, avalanche chutes and deep snow. Other photos and archival movie footage depict the utility of automobiles for passenger transport, hunting, freight hauling, woodcutting, racing, tourism and leisure throughout the vast frontier.

Although Alaska's automotive heritage is largely overshadowed by its aviation history, the automobile deserves recognition for the important role it played in the lives of our early pioneers. Fortunately, several of the Territory's earliest automobiles have been preserved and are on display in the Fountainhead Museum.

Top: This 1908 six-cylinder Franklin was the second car in Fairbanks and the first to reach the mining camp of Dome City. Photo courtesy of Candy Waugaman
Bottom: Early motorists traveling between Fairbanks and Valdez had to ford numerous glacial streams in the Alaska Range. As the day warmed the glaciers melted faster, and more than a few cars were stranded in the rising water. Photo courtesy of Frances Erickson
Left: A Chevrolet struggles through an avalanche chute along the Richardson Highway near Rainbow Ridge in 1928. Dorothy Loftus Collection 1980-84-162; Archives, University of Alaska Fairbanks

1905 SHELDON

Runabout

Alaska's first automobile was made by a 22-year-old who had never even seen a car!

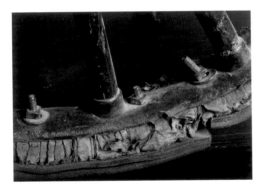

Of all the cars in the Fountainhead Collection, this one had the most romantic beginning. In 1905, Skagway resident Robert "Bobby" Sheldon wanted to impress a young lady and believed having an automobile would give him an advantage over her other suitor's horse and buggy. Although Sheldon had only seen pictures of cars in magazines and had limited access to materials, he believed he could build an auto that "would dazzle the young lady."

Sheldon built a wooden frame, attached four industrial cart wheels, salvaged a two-cycle marine engine from a sunken boat, added gears and built a chain drive. He made the tiller from sections of gas pipe and the seat from bar stools. Tin and oilcloth were fashioned into a hood and trunk cover. Reportedly, the 3.5-hp, one-cylinder engine could propel the car to a top speed of 15 mph. Unfortunately, the engine, most of the drive train and the carbide mining lamps Sheldon used for headlights were separated from the car many years ago.

Although there were very few roads in Skagway, Sheldon took the lady for many rides in his runabout. Did he marry her? "No," he said a number of years later, "but three other fellows have since then!"

Sheldon drove his little runabout in Skagway's Fourth-of-July parade in 1905 and was later showcased with it in the *Ripley's Believe It Or Not* newspaper feature. After moving to Fairbanks in 1908, Sheldon bought the town's first Model T in 1913, established an auto stage line between Fairbanks and the coast, and ultimately served in Alaska's first state legislature. In 1934, he donated his homemade car to the Alaska College Museum in Fairbanks. It is presently on loan from the University of Alaska Museum of the North.

FIRST AUTOMOBILE OF ALASKA. BUILT AT NORTH WEST LIGHT & POWER CO., SKAGWAY, ALASKA.

PHOTO COURTESY OF CANDY WAUGAMAN

A Man of Many Firsts.
Alaska Trailblazer
Robert Sheldon
1883 - 1983

TRAVEL

TOURISM

ALASKA ROAD COMMISSION

Sheldon's pioneering work in the transportation field made him well known and eventually led him to public service. Frustrated over Alaska's deplorable road conditions, he ran for and won a seat on the Alaska Road Commission. He also served two terms in the Territorial Legislature from 1925 to 1929, was appointed Fairbanks' postmaster and was elected to the first Alaska State Legislature in 1958.

1916 DODGE

1916 DODGE

Model 30-35 Touring

This is the very first Dodge shipped to Fairbanks. Pioneer Tom Gibson used it as a passenger stage between Fairbanks and Valdez.

Brothers John and Horace Dodge made a fortune as shareholders in, and suppliers to, the Ford Motor Company, but in 1914 they parted ways with Henry Ford and created a car of their own. The Dodge Brothers Model 30-35 was the first U.S. mass-produced auto with an all-steel body. Touted as a slightly more upscale competitor to the Ford Model T, it quickly gained a reputation for superb dependability. Its four-cylinder, inline L-head engine was so reliable that very few modifications were made to it over the next six years.

By the end of 1915 Dodge ranked fourth in U.S. auto sales (behind Ford, Willys-Overland and General Motors). The 1916 Dodge, introduced in July of 1915, was basically a continuation of the prior year's model. George S. Patton, then a lieutenant, used three Dodge touring cars to lead the first mechanized cavalry charge, against Pancho Villa's headquarters in the Sonora Desert in Mexico. An impressed General John J. Pershing ordered 250 more Dodges for his campaign against the infamous bandit.

Tom Gibson's Dodge, pictured above, is generously on loan from Don Cameron, Ray Cameron and David Stone.

SOURCES

General

Bailey, L. Scott and Richard M. Langworth (eds.). Automobile Quarterly's World of Cars. New York: L. Scott Bailey, 1971.

Clymer, Floyd. Those Wonderful Old Automobiles. New York: Bonanza Books, 1953.

Georgano. Nick (ed.). The Beaulieu Encyclopedia of the Automobile. Chicago: Fitzroy Dearborn Publishers, 2000.

Heasley, Jerry. The Production Figure Book for U.S. Cars. Minneapolis: Motorbooks International, 1977.

Kimes, Beverly Rae. Pioneers, Engineers and Scoundrels: The Dawn of the Automobile in America. Warrendale, PA: SAE International, 2005.

Kimes, Beverly Rae and Henry Austin Clark, Jr. Standard Catalog of American Cars: 1805-1942. Iola, WI: Krause, 1996.

Stein, Ralph. The American Automobile. New York: Random House, 1975.

Wager, Richard. Golden Wheels: The Story of the Automobiles Made in Cleveland and Northeastern Ohio. Cleveland: Western Reserve Historical Society & Cleveland Automobile Club, 1975.

1898 Hay Motor Vehicle

Brayton, Sean. "The Oldest Hay & Hotchkiss." The Horseless Carriage Gazette, May-June 2007.

Cuthbert, Bill." The Hay Gasoline Carriage." The Horseless Carriage Gazette, March-April 1989.

"Prospectus of the Walter Hay Company." Not dated.

"The Hay and Hotchkiss Co." The Horseless Age, October 1898.

"The Hay Gasoline Carriage." The Horseless Age, Vol. 5, No. 6, 8 November 1899.

1899 Hertel

Dolnar, Hugh. Motocycles of 1899," reprinted in American Machinist Memories: Selected Articles from early issues of American Machinist Magazine. Bradley, IL: Lindsay Publications, Inc., 1999.

Hiscox, Gardner D. Horseless Vehicles, Automobiles, Motor Cycles Operated by Steam, Hydro-carbon, Electric and Pneumatic Motors. New York: Munn and Company, 1900.

"The Hertel Automobile." The Automobile, Vol. II, No. 1, January 1900.

Factory literature

1903 Toledo

DeWitt, Nancy. "Fountainhead Antique Auto Museum." Horseless Carriage Gazette, Vol. 72, No. 2, March/April 2010.

"The Twelve Horsepower Toledo Touring Car." Horseless Age, Vol. 11, No. 16, 22 April 1903.

Factory Literature

1905 Sheldon

"Alaska's Auto Pioneer." Fairbanks Daily News-Miner, 18 July 2009.

"Bobby Sheldon is interviewed by Craig Smith in Fairbanks, Alaska in July

1975." Sound recording, UAF Oral History Archives, H75-18, July 1975.

"First Auto Made in Alaska Goes to Museum." Popular Mechanics, Vol. 63, No. 1, January 1936.

Pearson, Grant. My Life of High Adventure. Saddle River, NJ: Prentice-Hall, 1962.

Cole, Dermot. "Sheldon Demonstrated His Prized Wheels in July Fourth Parade." Fairbanks Daily News-Miner, 4 July 2005.

"The Travels of an Alaskan 'Stump Jumping' Ford." Ford Illustrated, Summer 1975.

1906 Cadillac

Hendry, Maurice. Cadillac: Standard of the World. New York: Bonanza Books, 1984.

Phillipi, Dick. "An Illustrated Technical History of the One-Cylinder Cadillac." Horseless Carriage Gazette, November-December 1961.

1906 Compound

Clough, Albert. "The Compound Light Touring Car." The Horseless Age, 11 October 1905.

Cuthbert, Bill. "A Dumbfounded Idea: The Compound Automobile." Bulb Horn, July 1993.

De Beaumont, P.S. "The Unusual Compound." Motorsport, date unknown.

Purdy, Ken. Motorcars of the Golden Past. New York: Little Brown, 1966.

Assorted sales literature, advertisements, and notes from the Harrah's Automobile Collection

1907 Cartercar

Brazeau, Mike. Cartercar. GM heritage Center, retrieved 2 January 2009 from http://history.gmheritagecenter. com/wiki/index.php/Cartercar

Dolnar, Hugh. "The 1907 Friction Drive 'Cartercar.'" Cycle and Automobile Trade Journal, Vol. XI, No. 8, February 1907.

Kimes, Beverly Rae. "A Few 'Whys' Worth Considering: Being a Narrative on the Cartercar; Telling of the Different Models, their Features and Advantages." Automobile Quarterly, Vol. 2, No. 2, 1974.

1907 Ford

Pate III, Carlton O. Pate's Early Ford Encyclopedia. Glastonbury, CT: Carlton O. Pate, 2008.

Vance, Bill. "Motoring Memories: Ford Model K, 1905-1908." www.canadiandriver.com

Factory literature

1907 Franklin

Katz, John F. "A Matter of Principle: The Wilkinson Era at Franklin." Automobile Quarterly, Vol. 26, No. 2, 1988.

Powell, Sinclair. The Franklin Automobile Company: The History of the Innovative Firm, Its Founders, the Vehicles It Produced (1902-1934), and the People Who Built Them. Warrendale, PA: Society of Automotive Engineers, 1999.

Powell, Sinclair and Mark H. Chaplin. Vintage Franklin: A History of the Car in Its Time. New York: H.H.

Franklin Club, Inc., 2007.

Factory literature

1907 White

Bromley, Michael L. William Taft and the First Motoring Presidency, 1909-1913. Jefferson, NC: McFarland Company, 2003.

Georgano, Nick. American Automobile: A Centenary 1893-1993. New York: Smithmark Publishers, 1992.

Weiant Jr., Warren S. "White Steam Car," Antique Automobile, May 1963.

1908 Rambler

Factory literature

1909 Hudson

Foster, Patrick. "The Birth of the Hudson: 1909-1929." Hemmings Classic Car, 1 November 2005.

Gunnell, John. "Twin 'H' Anniversaries." Old Cars Weekly, Vol. 38, No. 15, 9 April 2009.

Jackson, William S. "1909 Hudson 'Twenty' Roadster." Antique Automobile, Vol. 28, No. 5, September-October 1964.

Factory literature

1909 International

Historical Facts About Early International Harvester Automotive Vehicles: 1907-1947. Chicago: International Harvester Company, date unknown.

"The International Auto Buggy." The Horseless Age, Vol. 23, No. 6, 30 June 1909.

Factory literature

SOURCES

1909 Oldsmobile

Kimes, Beverly Rae (ed.). Oldsmobile: The First Seventy-five Years. New York: Princeton Publishing, 1978.

1910 Stanley

Foster, Kit. The Stanley Steamer: America's Legendary Steam Car. Estes Park, CO: The Stanley Museum, Inc., 2004.

"Stanley Motor Carriages Technical Information" and "The Stanley Steamer, Why the Fascination?" Retrieved on 23 October 2008 from stanleymotorcarriage.com.

Factory literature

1912 Peerless

Cope, Stanley P. "The Edwardian Peerless." Antique Automobile, Vol. 26, No. 2, March 1962.

Duerksen, Menno. "The Peerless Story: Part I." Cars & Parts, June 1995.

Hendry, Maurice. "The Peerless Story." Automobile Quarterly, Vol. 11 No. 1, 1973.

Orwig III, George. "Peerless: Part 1." Antique Automobile, Vol. 65, No. 1, January/February 2001.

Peerless Factory Announcement – 1912 Models (factory lit)

1912 Premier

Cuthbert, Bill. "Premier: The Quality Car." The Horseless Carriage Gazette, March-April 1990.

MacIlvain, Walter O. "The Premier." Bulb Horn, July-August 1976.

"Premier Builds '4-40' and '6-60'." The Automobile, June 1911.

"Premier 1911." Cycle and Automobile Trade Journal, Vol. 15, No. 6, December 1910.

"The Premier Six." Automobile Trade Journal, Vol. 16, No. 12, June 1912.

Nethercutt Museum records, sales literature

1913-14 Rauch & Lang

Rauch & Lang. Retrieved on 7 April 2008 from http://www.coachbuilt.com/bui/b/baker_raulang/baker_raulang.htm

Correspondence with the Antique Electric Vehicle Forum

1914 Moline-Knight

"Moline Brings Out Low-Priced Knight-Motored Car." Automobile Trade Journal, Vol. 18, No. 7, January 1914.

"Moline Has Knight Motor." The Automobile, 20 November 1913.

"Moline-Knight Breaks All Endurance Records." The Horseless Age, 7 January 1914.

"Moline 1914 Cars with New Design of Knight Motor." The Horseless Age, Vol. 32, No. 22, 26 November 1913.

"Moline-Knight Characterized by Unusual Motor Details." Motor Age, 20 November 1913.

"Moline-Knight Enters the Lists." Automobile Topics, 22 November 1913.

"Moline-Knight Test Establishes a New Record." Automobile Trade Journal, Vol. 18, No. 8, February 1914.

Moline/R&V Car Registry; factory literature

1914 Woods Mobilette

Cunningham, Robert D. Orphan Babies: America's Forgotten Economy Cars, Volume I, 1887-1927. Des Moines, IA: Cunningham Studio, 2008.

"Cyclecar Craze Peaked by World War I." Old Cars News & Marketplace, 18 November 1993.

Knouff, Lorentz B. "Woods Mobilette." Antique Automobile, January-February 1968.

1917 Model T Snow Flyer

"A Brief History of the Model T Ford Snowmobile." Retrieved on 23 March 2009 from the Model T Ford Snowmobile Club, www.modeltfordsnowmobile.com.

Amsden, Roger. "Model-T Snowmobiles Coming Home to Birthplace." Retrieved on 12 March 2009 from the Winnipesaukee Forum, http://www.winnipesaukee.com/forums/showthread.php?t=1507

Brooke, Lindsay. "An Original Snowmobile." The New York Times, 14 January 2009. http://ossipeelake.org/news/2009/01/15/an-original-snowmobile/

Campbell, Stephen. "History of Snowmobiling." 2006. Retrieved on 12 March 2009 from http://www.millinocket-maine.net/history-of-snowmobiling.htm

1917 Owen Magnetic

Duerksen, Menno. "The Story of the Entz Magnetic Clutch and the Owen-Magnetic Motor Car." Cars & Parts, April 1975.

Wells, Stuart W. "Car of a Thousand Speeds: The Entz System and Owen Magnetic." Automobile Quarterly, Vol. 36, No. 3, 1997.

Zahm, Karl S. "Owen & Entz: An Electrifying Combination – The Story of Owen Magnetic Part I." Bulb Horn, January-March 1991.

Zahm, Karl S. "Owen & Entz: An Electrifying Combination – The Story of Owen Magnetic Part II." Bulb Horn, April-June 1991.

Zahm, Karl S. "Owen & Entz: An Electrifying Combination – The Story of Owen Magnetic Part III." Bulb Horn, July-September 1991.

Sales literature

1917 Pierce-Arrow

Brierley, Brooks T. There is No Mistaking a Pierce-Arrow. Coconut Grove, FL: Garrett and Stringer, Inc., 1979.

Weis, Bernard. The Pierce-Arrow Motor Car. Cedar Rapids, IA: Pierce-Arrow Society, 1981.

1918 Stutz

Katzell, Raymond (ed.). The Splendid Stutz. Pennsauken, NJ: Turning Point Press, 1996.

"H.C.S. and Bulldog Are Latest Additions to Stutz Line." Motor Age, September 1914.

Peck, Cameron. "Stutz." Automobile Quarterly, Vol. 2, No. 1, 1963.

"Stutz." The Motor Age, 4 January 1917.

"Stutz." The Motor Age, 3 January 1918.

"Stutz." Undated clipping from Cars & Parts.

1919 Studebaker

Brierley, Brooks T. "The Studebaker Big Six." Hemmings Classic Car, November 2007.

Moloney, James. Studebaker Cars. Minneapolis: Motorbooks International, 1994.

1920 Argonne

Baeke, John (ed.). The Reunion: Number Two. Auburn, IN: Auburn Cord Duesenberg Club, 2010.

Naul, G. Marshall. "The Argonne: Power and Speed With Economy." Automotive History Review, Vol. 1, No. 1, 1974.

"New Cars and Models: Argonne High-Speed Runabout." Automobile Trade Journal, Vol. 23, No. 1, July 1919.

Roe, Fred. "The After Life of the Argonne." Automotive History Review, No. 7, Fall 1977.

"American Sports Cars—Duesenberg-Powered." Undated clipping from Modern Motor Car.

"Specifications for the 'Argonne Four' Special Roadster," notes from Harrah's Automobile Collection.

1921 Daniels

Brierley, Brooks T. "Discovering the Daniels." The Classic Car, Fall 2009.

"Daniels Eight is Interesting Example of Detailed Refinement." Automobile Trade Journal, Vol. 21, No. 12, June 1917.

"Daniels Eight of Strong Construction." The Automobile, October 1915.

Hafer, Erminie Shaeffer. A Century of Vehicle Craftsmanship. Boyertown, PA: The Hafer Foundation, 1972.

Leman, Jim. "Distinguished Daniels Was Very Short Lived." Daily Herald, Arlington Heights, Il 14 August 2006.

Summers, Fred. "Daniels Live." Classic Car Club of America Bulletin, May 2010.

Correspondence with the Boyertown Museum of Historic Vehicles, Boyertown Pennsylvania

1921 Heine-Velox

Cooper, Dan. "V-12 Power!" February 2005. http://www.suite101.com/

article.cfm/vintage_classic_
cars/114383

"History and Features of the San
Francisco Built Heine-Velox Car."
Motor West, January 1921.

"New High-Priced Twelve." Automotive
Industries, January 1921.

Purdy, Ken. Motorcars of the Golden
Past. New York: Galahad Books,
1966.

"The Heine-Velox Car." The Automobile,
February 1906.

Tikker, Kevin Scott. Heine-Velox, The
Forgotten Car From San Francisco.
Unpublished manuscript, 1981.

Tikker, Kevin Scott. "Gustav Heine
and His Cars." Automotive History
Review, No. 15, Fall 1982.

Tikker, Kevin Scott. "The Migration of
the Heine-Velox." Automotive History
Review, No. 15, Fall 1982.

Original glass plates, photographs and
notes from the Gustav Heine estate.

1922 Wills Sainte Claire

Hendry, Maurice D. "Wills Sainte Claire:
The Gray Goose and its founder." Car
Classics, June 1978.

Stevens, Bob. "Wills Sainte Claire."
Undated clipping from Cars & Parts.

Factory Literature

1927 Stutz

Emanuel, Dave. "Drift, Salvation,
Malaise: The Stutz Motor Car
Company of America." Automobile
Quarterly, Vol. 20, No. 3, 1982.

Katzell, Raymond, editor. The Splendid
Stutz. Pennsauken, NJ: Turning Point
Press, 1996.

Petersen, West. "Economy, Safety,

Innovation and Scandal." Stutz
News, July-September 2003.

Petrik, James F. "Black Hawk??…Or
Blackhawk??" Stutz News, April-
June 1989.

1931 Cord

Burger, Dan. "The L-29 Cord: Style
and Innovation in Dramatic
Combination." Antique Automobile,
January-February 1981.

Huntington, Roger. The Cord Front-
Drive: The Intriguing Story of a
Fabulous Automobile. Los Angeles:
Floyd Clymer Publications, 1957.

Post, Dan. Cord - Without Tribute to
Tradition: The L-29 Front-Drive
Legend. Arcadia, CA: Post Era
Publications, 1974.

Factory literature

1932 Cadillac

Albert, Ken. Who Won the Multi-
Cylinder War?" The Classic Car, Vol.
LVIII, No. 2, Summer 2010.

Borgeson, Griffith. "'The Engine of
Engines, to Power the Car of Cars':
The OHV Cadillac V-16 Engine."
Automobile Quarterly, Vol. 22, No.
4, 1984.

Borgeson, Griffith. "Marmon's
Masterpieces." Automobile
Quarterly, Vol. 27, No. 2, 1989.

Hendry, Maurice. Cadillac: Standard
of the World. New York: Bonanza
Books, 1984.

Nerad, Jack. "Cadillac V-16." Driving
Today, http://www.drivingtoday.com/
greatest_cars/cadillacv16/index.
html.

Saunders, Yann. "The Cadillac V-16."

Retrieved from The Cadillac
Database on 26 February 2009 from
http://www.cadillacdatabase.org.

Schneider, Roy. Sixteen Cylinder
Motorcars: An Illustrated History.
Arcadia, CA: Heritage House, 1974.

Factory literature

1932 Chrysler

Adler, Dennis. The Nethercutt
Collection: The Cars of San
Sylmar. Minneapolis: Blue Book
Publications, 2004.

Brown, Arch. "Classic Chrysler: 1932
Custom Imperial." Special Interest
Autos, No. 105, June 1988.

Brown, Arch. "Low-Priced Elegance:
1932 Chrysler Imperial Series CH
Convertible Sedan." Cars & Parts,
April 1992.

Dammann, George. 70 Years of
Chrysler. Sarasota, FL: Crestline
Publishing, 1974.

Heppensteele, Lee B. "Imperial:
Dowager Queen of Chrysler
Corporation." Antique Automobile,
Vol. 34, No. 3, May-June 1970.

Shinstine, Doug and Gail Shinstine.
"1932 Chrysler Imperial CL
Convertible Sedan, LeBaron."
Bumper Guardian, June 2006.

1933 Auburn

Arch Brown. "1933 Auburn Salon
Twelve: Phenomenal Phaeton."
Special Interest Autos No. 109, Feb,
1989.

Kimes, Beverly Rae. "Auburn: From
Runabout to Speedster." Automobile
Quarterly, Vol. 5, No. 4, 1967.

Research Report from the Auburn Cord

Duesenberg Museum, 7 March, 2006.

1933 Hupmobile

Godshall, Jeff. "Cycle-Fendered Hupp:
The Ugly Duckling That Became the
Beautiful Swan." Special-Interest
Autos, November-December 1976.

Duerksen, Menno. "The Story of
Hupmobile – Part IV." Undated
clipping from Cars & Parts.

1934 American Austin

"American Austin was a licensed
version of the Seven." Retrieved on
2 August 2009 from http://www.
austinbantamclub.com.

Cunningham, Robert D. Orphan Babies:
America's Forgotten Economy Cars,
Volume 2, 1927-1943. Des Moines,
IA: Cunningham Studio, 2008.

Domer, George Edward. "Good Things
Did Come in Small Packages."
Automobile Quarterly, Vol. 14, No.
4, 1976.

Foster, Kit. "Butler's Babies." The
Automobile, February 2003.

Foster, Kit. "Austin Power," Kit Foster's
Carport, June 2007, http://www.
kitfoster.com/carport/2007/06/
austin-power/.

Kloepfer, Donald. "The Austin in
America." Retrieved on 4 November
2009 from http://www.oldmotors.
com/ftr-austin.htm

Nerad, Jack. "Austin 7." Driving Today,
http://www.drivingtoday.com/
greatest_cars/austin7/index.html.

Vance, Bill. "1938 American Austin/
Bantam: 1937-1940." Retrieved on 2
August 2009 from http://www.autos.
ca/classic-cars/motoring-memories-

american-austinbantam-1937-1940.

1936 Packard

Kimes, Beverly Rae (ed.). Packard:
A History of the Motorcar and
the Company. New Albany, IN:
Automobile Heritage Publishing and
Communications, 2002.

Midget Racers

Fox, Jack C. The Mighty Midgets.
Speedway, IN: Carl Hungness
Publishing, 1977.

Frazer, Dustin. "The Roar of the Mighty
Midgets." Stock Car Racing, October
and November 1969.

Gudaitis, Frank. "The Outboards." Open
Wheel Magazine, April 1983.

Gudaitis, Frank. "Swanson's Song."
Circle Track, July 1987.

Gudaitis, Frank. "The Early Outboard
Midgets." Vintage Motor Sport, July/
Aug 1990.

"John Homan and Ralph Moody."
Retrieved on 5 April 2009 from
http://www.mshf.com/hof/holman_
moody.htm

Modestino, Lou. "Ralph Moody." Stock
Car Racing, July 1968.

Watson, Ed. Midget Auto Racing:
The First 70 Years. Marshall, IN:
Walsworth Publishing, 2003.

Webb, W.J. "I Remember Elto." The
Antique Outboarder, July 1972.

White, Gordon. Offenhauser: The
Legendary Racing Engine and the
Men Who Built It. Osceola, WI:
Motorbooks International, 1996.

Wilkins, Ed and Eddie Hitze. "The Elto
4-60." The Antique Outboarder, July
1970.

ACKNOWLEDGMENTS

Bobby Sheldon shortened the axles of his Model Ts so the tires would fit in the narrower tracks made by the horse-drawn sleighs still traveling the Valdez-Fairbanks Trail. Photo courtesy of Frances Erickson

It has been my privilege to serve as the historian for the Fountainhead Antique Auto Museum, and I am indebted to Tim and Barbara Cerny for allowing me to work with such an extraordinary collection of artifacts. I am also grateful to our museum manager, Willy Vinton, for his willingness to reposition cars for photographs and answer my countless questions.

Several organizations and institutions helped me track down valuable information pertaining to the car marques represented in the Fountainhead Collection. Roberta Watkins with the Horseless Carriage Club Foundation Library and Chris Ritter with the AACA Library & Research Center were especially helpful and quick to respond to my requests. I also benefited greatly from the archives at the Benson Ford Research Center, Nethercutt Automotive Research Library, Boyertown Museum of Historic Vehicles and the National Automotive History Collection at the Detroit Public Library. I am also indebted to J. Parker Wickham for access to his personal library.

Special thanks go to those who generously loaned cars to our museum and allowed us to include them in this book: the University of Alaska Museum of the North for the 1905 Sheldon, and Don Cameron, Ray Cameron and David Stone for the 1916 Dodge.

I thoroughly enjoyed working with Ronn Murray Photography to obtain the majority of the photographs for this book. Ronn's skill, artistic flare and sincere enthusiasm for classic cars were a perfect match for this project. Ronn and I appreciated the assistance provided by Rod Benson, Charlie Jurgin, Michael Lecorchik, Scott Grundy and Kristen Summerlin during the photography sessions. Many thanks also to Deanna Brandon, Cass Cerny and Jody Thomas Photography for providing photographs for this book.

I am grateful to Candy Waugaman for allowing me access to her vast collection of vintage Alaska photographs, regaling me with historic anecdotes and connecting me with other beneficial resources. Frances Erickson generously shared photographs, newspaper clippings and colorful memories of her father, Robert "Bobby" Sheldon. I also made use of a treasure trove of archived photographs, videos and newspapers in the Elmer E. Rasmuson Library at the University of Alaska Fairbanks.

It was a terrific pleasure to work with my editor, John Katz. His manuscript improvements, personal encouragement and vast knowledge of automotive history added considerably to this book. John's willingness to travel to Fairbanks during the height of winter is to be applauded.

Despite his remarkable lack of interest in old cars, my husband Jim cheered my efforts, tolerated my late nights at the keyboard and digitally restored the old photographs used in this book. I am forever grateful for the loving support he provides, no matter what intriguing career I pursue.

Nancy DeWitt
Fairbanks, Alaska

SUBJECT INDEX

Top: Fairbanks garden party. PHOTO COURTESY OF CANDY WAUGAMAN   **Bottom: Repairing the rear end of a Ford Model T on the tundra of the Alaska Range.** PHOTO COURTESY OF FRANCES ERICKSON

Bobby Sheldon equipped his Model Ts with skis, chains and sometimes even a caterpillar track for winter travel. The front-mounted fuel tank allowed gas to continue flowing to the engine even when the car climbed steep grades. PHOTO COURTESY OF FRANCES ERICKSON

WEDGEWOOD RESORT

HOME OF THE FOUNTAINHEAD ANTIQUE AUTO MUSEUM

Wedgewood Resort is a destination in itself. This beautiful property includes Bear Lodge, residential suites and a private nature preserve, all conveniently situated near downtown Fairbanks and adjacent to the 2,000-acre Creamer's Field Migratory Waterfowl Refuge.

There is no shortage of things to do at Wedgewood Resort. Peruse Alaska art and photographic exhibits lining the hallways, lobby and the convention center. Stroll past breath-taking flower displays, historic artifacts and interpretive exhibits that line the resort's walkways. Learn how plants and animals survive Alaska's extreme climate by exploring the self-guided nature trails at the 75-acre Wedgewood Wildlife Sanctuary. Relax on the observation decks overlooking Wander Lake or try your luck in the photography blind. Check out the exhibits, library and bird feeders at the Alaska Bird Observatory. After dinner at the Golden Bear Restaurant, take in one of the resort's evening presentations. You might just meet an owl!

Undoubtedly, the most fascinating attraction at Wedgewood Resort is the Fountainhead Antique Auto Museum. This remarkable collection of automobiles, historic clothing and vintage Alaska photographs is just a short walk or free shuttle ride from any building on the resort's campus. On most summer evenings, one of the museum cars cruises around the hotel grounds, much to the delight of visitors. A stay at Wedgewood Resort supports the continued preservation, exhibition and operation of these historic vehicles. In return, hotel guests receive discounted admission to the museum.

For more information about Wedgewood Resort, visit www.fountainheadhotels.com or call 1-800-528-4916.